FOOD AND DRINK
IN ANGLO-SAXON ENGLAND

DEBBY BANHAM

TEMPUS

First published 2004

Tempus Publishing Limited
The Mill, Brimscombe Port,
Stroud, Gloucestershire, GL5 2QG
www.tempus-publishing.com

British Library Cataloguing in Publication Data.
A catalogue record for this book is available from the British Library.

ISBN 0 7524 2909 4

Typesetting and origination by Tempus Publishing Limited
Printed in Great Britain by Midway Colour Print, Wiltshire.

FOOD AND DRINK
IN ANGLO-SAXON ENGLAND

CONTENTS

00080156990010

ACKNOWLEDGEMENTS

First of all, I'd like to thank the other worker in the field of Anglo-Saxon diet, Ann Hagen, for many fruitful discussions on our subject. I also owe a debt of gratitude to Dr Jane Renfrew, who supervised the thesis on which this book is partly based, and Professor Ray Page, who advised me in its early stages.

More recently, the work I've done with Dr Ros Faith on Anglo-Saxon farming has influenced my thinking on diet and everyday life. I'd also like to thank the members of the Medieval Diet Group for their comments on my work, as well as the scholars who responded to my papers at the first Anglo-Saxon Plant Names congress in Glasgow in 2000 and the conferences on 'The Table' at Sheffield and 'Cross and Crucifix in Anglo-Saxon England and on the Continent' at Winchester in 2003, not to mention participants at several International Medieval Congresses at Leeds.

I'm very grateful to Suffolk County Council Archaeology Service, in the person of Keith Wade, for generous help with illustrations, and to Peter Murphy, who gave me permission to quote from his AML report. I'd also like to thank Laura Sole and the staff at Bede's World for letting me take photos of their crops and livestock, and discussing with me the running of their 'Anglo-Saxon' farm.

And I must thank my partner, Frank Goodingham, for help with photography and driving. I should also thank him, as well as Mary Corbett, Julie Crick and Anna Kendrew, for putting up with my distracted behaviour with such good humour.

INTRODUCTION
How, What, Why?

This book originates in my student daydreams. Sitting in lectures about Anglo-Saxon kings and bishops, I used to think 'Yes, very interesting, but what did they have for breakfast before they fought the battle, or reformed the church?' I wanted to know what it was *like* to be an Anglo-Saxon, irrespective of whatever momentous events were going on at the time. None of the books I read, however fascinating, dealt with these questions. In fact, the answers still elude me, but the first question set me off on a research career that has produced, among other things, this book. Even now, it is impossible to say with any confidence what the Anglo-Saxons ate at each meal, but I do at least know what their overall diet consisted of, in terms of crops, livestock, wild and imported foods, and I know something about the cooking and preservation techniques they had at their disposal. So progress has been made: I know what they *could* have had for breakfast. (See the last chapter for some shameless speculation on this score.)

Food clearly played an important part in Anglo-Saxon life. Not only did it keep people alive, it also marked all the important occasions in their lives. In the great epic poem *Beowulf*, victory is celebrated by feasting, and there can be no doubt that this happened in real life as well. Kings also held feasts on all the great religious festivals, to which their most important subjects were invited, and at which the business of state was enacted. At a humbler level, landlords provided feasts for their tenants and workers after the harvest and other major agricultural tasks. Funerals – and probably weddings and christenings too – were followed by feasting. And no doubt every household celebrated the turning points of the year with a feast, each according to its wealth and status, and the success or otherwise of the year's bread-winning.[1]

Despite the obvious significance of food and eating in Anglo-Saxon society, the major written sources tell us remarkably little about either. With the exception of some funeral feasts at Bury St Edmunds, we have no idea what was eaten at any of these meals.[2] *Beowulf* tells us what was drunk, but food is not even mentioned, despite the occasion being described as a feast. Old English literature is simply not interested in eating. Nor is Anglo-Saxon government documentation – law-codes and charters – but it does concern itself with the support of the ruling classes, in the form of food rents (Old English *feorm*). These are prescribed in some detail, listing the products of their labours, with quantities, that tenants had to supply to their landlord. By the end of the period, many food rents had been commuted into money payments, but others were still being paid in kind at the time of the Domesday Book inquest in 1086. From the later Anglo-Saxon period we also have a small body of estate management literature: *Rectitudines singularum personarum* ('The rights of different people'), *Be gesceadwisan gerefan* ('On the prudent steward'), and

1 *Earl Harold Godwinson and his companions feasting, probably at his estate at Bosham, Sussex, before setting out for France in 1064 or 1065, from the Bayeux Tapestry. It is difficult to tell what they are eating, but splendid drinking vessels are prominently displayed*

8

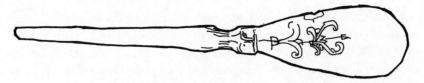

2 *Bone spoon, 18.6cm long, from Winchester, probably early eleventh century. Most Anglo-Saxon spoons were rather less fancy than this. They were made from wood, and probably horn, as well as bone. Now in Winchester Museum.* After Janet Backhouse *et al.*, The Golden Age of Anglo-Saxon Art, British Museum 1984

the group of 'farming memoranda' from the abbey at Ely.[3] All these mention foodstuffs, as well as other agricultural products. In Ælfric's *Colloquy*, a set of dialogues written around the year 1000 to teach monastic pupils Latin, each boy plays the part of a different worker, most of them concerned with food production in some way.[4]

We have some textual evidence for food production, then, but, apart from the Bury funeral feasts, only two texts deal with its consumption, both from a monastic *milieu*. They are the *Monasteriales indicia*, the Old English sign language, for use when monks had to keep silence, including at meals, and Ælfric's *Colloquy* again.[5] The *Indicia* lists signs for foods, drinks and other items belonging to the refectory, and in the *Colloquy*, one of the boys tells the master what he has to eat and drink each day. Both texts come from the end of our period, after the great Benedictine reform of the tenth century, so they may not even be a good guide to what monks ate before that, let alone the population at large. Nevertheless, both give quite comprehensive lists, and because we know what the restrictions were on monastic diet, we can be reasonably confident about how it differed from that of the contemporary lay population. Neither of these texts includes recipes, but a few are given in the Old English medical texts, *Bald's Leechbook, Leechbook III*, and the *Lacnunga*.[6] Of course, the vast majority of the recipes in these texts are for medicaments, but the ones that concern us here deal with invalid food, rather than medicine proper. Some of these are given in the final chapter. The problem with these recipes is that they are intended for patients suffering from particular illnesses, and we have no way of knowing if healthy Anglo-Saxons would eat the same things. Apart from these texts, our textual evidence for what was eaten in Anglo-Saxon England is confined to incidental references, mostly in saints' lives. The most famous story about an Anglo-Saxon and food, that of King Alfred and the cakes, is first recorded in the twelfth century, so unfortunately it cannot be used as evidence for diet before the Norman Conquest.[7]

Luckily, we do not rely entirely on texts for our knowledge of Anglo-Saxon diet. Archaeology can provide us with a good deal of information. First of all, objects are often found on archaeological sites that were used in the production and processing of food: ploughs, mills, cooking pots, and of course the ubiquitous remains of fires. Consumption, too, leaves its artefacts, notably drinking vessels and the knives which all Anglo-Saxons seem to have carried with them. Although these artefacts might seem fairly robust, many of them do not survive well in the soil. This is especially true of those made of organic materials such as wood or textiles, but even the iron of knives can be reduced to a mass of rust after a thousand years or more. This means that the artefacts most commonly found in archaeology may not have been the most common in use, only made of the most durable materials. Some of the most basic equipment is virtually unknown in the archaeological record: for instance, wooden bowls are only found on waterlogged sites, mainly at York,[8] and only two or three Anglo-Saxon spoons are known, apart from ceremonial ones.

Secondly, there are the remains of the actual foodstuffs eaten by the people who lived on the site. Except in very acid soils, animal bones are found on nearly all habitation sites, frequently with cut marks from the butcher's knife or cleaver to demonstrate that the flesh was eaten.[9] However, they do not necessarily provide a full picture of the range of animals eaten at the site, because small bones, whether those of young animals, small types of animal such as fish and birds, or the smaller bones of larger animals, are less likely to be preserved than large ones like the long bones of cattle and horses. The remains of plant foods are less commonly found, but there is now a substantial body of records of both pollen and macroscopic remains (i.e. those large enough to be seen without a microscope), mainly seeds.[10] Macroscopic remains usually survive only in waterlogged deposits in Britain, but pollen is preserved in a wider range of conditions. While some plant remains are found in 'latrine deposits', where there is little doubt that they have passed through the human digestive system, we have to be very cautious about assuming that other finds formed part of the diet. The seeds of wild plants, for instance, can be found in huge numbers where they have been growing as weeds. Only where we know from other evidence that the plant concerned was regarded as edible can we be reasonably sure that its remains represent food.

We also have linguistic evidence, mostly from place names. The names of plants frequently occur in place names, and sometimes those of animals, such as oxen at Oxford. Plant and animal names in place names tell us not only that the species involved was found at a particular place, but also that for some reason it was remarkable enough to identify that place. For instance, 'Appleton's in the north of England (and names in 'pear'- in the south) may have been the only places in their neighbourhoods where that fruit could be gathered, being at the northern edge of its natural range. 'Banham' could have been the only local farm or village to grow beans before they became a standard part of the cropping regime, or maybe it grew particularly good ones. The problem with place names, however, is dating. The number for which we have evidence from within the Anglo-Saxon period is pretty small. Many more are recorded in Domesday Book, and most of these must have already been current before the Conquest. But place names can change, so we cannot be certain. Place name scholars have proposed various chronologies, suggesting that different types of place name (those in *–tun* and those in *–ham*, for instance) were coined in a particular order. None of these has gained universal acceptance, however, so it would be unwise to rely on any of them to date the origin of an individual name.[11]

Other linguistic evidence can be found in the vocabulary of Old English.[12] For instance, 'walnut' comes from OE *wealhnutu* (literally 'foreign nut'), suggesting that these nuts were known in Anglo-Saxon England, but were either imported or not common enough in cultivation to be accepted as 'English'. By the time they became more common, the name had stuck. Again, one of the Old English words for a vegetable garden was *lectun* ('leek enclosure'), suggesting that leeks were the most familiar Anglo-Saxon vegetable, and may indeed have been the only thing that some people grew in their gardens. But the meaning of words is extremely fluid, being determined only by usage, and we have to take into account the fact that it may not be possible to translate an Old English or Latin word exactly by a modern English one. For instance, onions and garlic count as types of leek in Old English (*garleac*, literally 'spear-leek', giving us the modern word in the latter case), so the 'leeks' grown in the vegetable garden could have included things that we would count as quite distinct plants.

Finally, there is the evidence of the visual arts: although frequently attractive, paintings and sculpture are difficult to use as evidence for real life in Anglo-Saxon England.[13] For instance, the appearance of vine-scroll ornament on Northumbrian cross-shafts tells us nothing about Anglo-Saxon viticulture (especially in Northumbria); the motif is borrowed from sub-classical Mediterranean art, and no doubt refers to Christ as the 'true vine', as well as to the eucharistic use of wine (see **colour plate 2**). And 'inhabited vine-scroll' certainly cannot tell us what animals inhabited Anglo-Saxon England (see **colour plate 3**). Even the illustrations in the Old English illuminated *Herbarium*, although undoubtedly derived from pictures provided for identification purposes, cannot have functioned in this way themselves.[14] Some are simply unrecognisable as the plants they purport to represent, but, more importantly, as Professor M.A. D'Aronco has shown, all of them are derived from recognised traditions of sub-classical herbal illustration on the Continent. None of them, therefore, was drawn from an Anglo-Saxon plant.

All these sources of information clearly have their difficulties, but we need not be daunted. Between them they present us with a pretty substantial amount of information, and by combining them we can often overcome the uncertainties that might bedevil any single type of evidence. There will always be some questions that the evidence simply refuses to answer for us – for instance, it may never be possible to establish with any precision at what times of day Anglo-Saxon lay people ate their meals – but, when there is so much that we can be reasonably sure about, it would be idle to waste time worrying about what we cannot know. Overall, we can present a very full picture of what the Anglo-Saxons ate, what they could produce themselves, what they gathered from the wild, what they imported, how they stored and cooked it, even in some cases what they ate with what, and what they liked and what they turned their noses up at.

—❧ ONE ❧—

THE STAFF OF LIFE
Cereals, Bread and Beer

Cereals – wheat, barley, and to a lesser extent oats and rye – were by far the most important element in the Anglo-Saxon diet. People may have valued animal foods more highly, but grains, in one form or another, were what they mostly ate and drank, and the majority of their nutrients must have come from cereal sources as a result. Cereals are the nearest there is to a complete food, containing protein, fat and many vitamins, as well as providing plenty of calories.[1] As long as some fresh plant foods are also available to supply vitamin C, one can live almost entirely on barley or wheat, for instance. This is undoubtedly why various grains have been the staple foods of nearly all cultures throughout human history. They also have the advantage of being a concentrated source of nourishment, since they contain little moisture; and, for the same reason, they store well and are therefore available all year round as long as supplies do not run out. Many different techniques of preparation and cooking can be applied to cereals, and their versatility is one reason that they are still staple foods for most people, even in modern societies with almost limitless choice.

Because they formed the bulk of the Anglo-Saxon diet, we have more evidence, both written and archaeological, from the period for cereals than for any other kind of food. This means it is possible to detect changes in the cereal part of the diet over the course of the Anglo-Saxon period, and make at least some informed guesses about varying customs in different parts of England. One major change is readily apparent from the archaeological evidence: at the beginning of the Anglo-Saxon period, barley was the grain most commonly grown in England, but the balance began to shift later on, so that by the time of the Norman Conquest, more wheat was being grown than barley.[2] The bulk of this increase was accounted for by types of wheat suitable for making bread, such as *Triticum aestivum* var. *aestivum*. These are free-threshing, or naked, wheats, meaning that all the chaff can be removed from the grain by threshing, winnowing, and possibly sieving. Hulled wheats, such as spelt, which have to be roasted or parched to remove the inner chaff before they can be ground, were also grown, but they were not so common, and if anything declined in popularity as the period wore on. It may be therefore that the main change was in the grain that people used to make bread. The Anglo-Saxons certainly preferred wheaten to barley bread (see below), and it may be that the improving climatic conditions of the tenth century onwards allowed more of them to gratify this preference.[3]

It is not always possible to tell the archaeological remains of one species of wheat from another, or even from other cereals if they are not well preserved, and, on top of this, the classification of wheat has changed in recent years, so that older reports may be misleading. In spite of these difficulties, it is at least possible to list the types of grain grown in Anglo-Saxon England and, more tentatively, their relative abundance.[4] *Triticum aestivum* var. *aestivum*, bread wheat, was probably the most common of the free-threshing types, but *T. aestivum* var. *compactum*, club wheat, was also grown. The main hulled wheat was spelt (*T. aestivum* var. *spelta*), which had been a common cereal in Roman Britain, and emmer (*T. turgidum* var. *dicoccum*) may also have been grown. As noted above, these were never as widespread as free-threshing wheats but they do continue to appear right through the period. Although the amount of barley (*Hordeum vulgare*) being grown declined, it remained the second most common cereal throughout the period. It is likely that some barley bread continued to be made, however

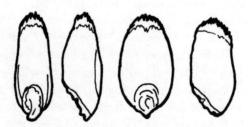

3 *Grains of spelt* (Triticum aestivum *var.* spelta)*, the main hulled wheat grown in Anglo-Saxon England, and bread wheat* (Triticum aestivum *var.* aestivum)*. Spelt would only appear naked like this after extensive processing, whereas grains of bread wheat would thresh free and only require winnowing to get rid of the chaff.* After Renfrew, Palaeoethnobotany

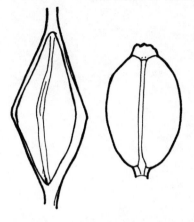

4 *Barley (*Hordeum vulgare*), hulled and naked grains. As with wheat, hulled barley requires a great deal of processing before it can be made into bread, but is preferred for malting, and is thus the most widely grown type at the present day. Barley remained popular throughout the Anglo-Saxon period, although its use for bread is likely to have declined. After Renfrew,* Palaeoethnobotany

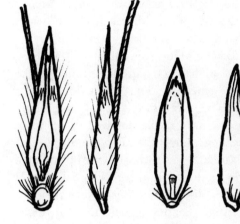

5 *Wild (left) and cultivated oats (*Avena fatua *and* A. sativa *respectively). The lemma of wild oat is very hairy, compared with the cultivated variety, and the awn very robust. However, the grains inside are much harder to tell apart. After Renfrew,* Palaeoethnobotany

unpopular it was. Barley would also be cooked in other ways (see below), and it was always needed for brewing. Most varieties of barley are hulled, which makes them difficult to use for bread, but better for malting, which may help to explain the changing role of this cereal in Anglo-Saxon England. Remains of oats, *Avena* species, and rye, *Secale cereale*, are also found on Anglo-Saxon sites. Neither seems to have been as popular as wheat or barley, and in the case of oats we cannot always be sure that it was being cultivated deliberately, and not growing as a weed in a crop of some other cereal. The wild oat, *Avena fatua*, is an ancestor of the cultivated species *A. sativa*, and thus it is hard to distinguish the grains of the two, especially after they have been in the ground for a thousand years. Rye also began as a weed, and both cereals can grow in conditions unsuitable for wheat and barley. They may have been grown as an 'insurance crop' in case the preferred cereals failed.

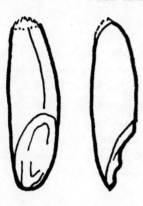

6 *Rye* (Secale cereale). *Compare figs 3–5.* After Renfrew, *Palaeoethnobotany*

Most of our evidence comes from sites in lowland England, and so we are not able to say much about how upland areas may have differed. A recent survey by Jacqueline Huntley of early medieval sites in northern England and Scotland shows that bread wheat and barley were also popular in these more challenging parts of Britain.[5] However, oats are also frequent on these sites, and many upland areas still have a tradition of eating oatcakes in the modern period, and did not generally adopt wheat flour until it became available commercially. This is because wheat is a fussy crop, requiring a relatively long growing season and a fertile but well-drained soil, whereas other cereals are much less demanding. Oats in particular are tolerant of 'moist maritime climates'.[6] Like Wales and Scotland, upland areas of England probably changed fairly gradually from barley to oats as their main bread-corn during the course of the Middle Ages. Nevertheless, it would not be accurate to divide Anglo-Saxon England into an upland zone, growing oats and barley, and a lowland one growing wheat, as was possible in the early modern period, because, even in the later Middle Ages, many areas in the south and east (Essex, for instance) grew mainly oats, and were considered unsuitable for the cultivation of wheat.[7]

BREAD

In many countries, the use of a staple cereal food defines both a sense of national identity and a 'proper' meal. Emiko Ohnuki-Tierney has written that, for the Japanese, '*manpukukan* (the full-stomach feeling) is not achieved without rice, no matter what else is eaten'.[8] She compares a meal without rice for a Japanese person to 'sandwiches for dinner for many Americans'. For 'Americans' here, she could just as well have written 'Britons'. Until recently, most British people would not have felt *man-*

pukukan unless they had eaten potatoes – bread implied, and still implies, a snack or a light meal. However, this was not the case in Anglo-Saxon England (or, I suspect, in any part of Britain until potatoes were introduced); a proper meal meant bread, although not of course on its own. One of the very few pieces of evidence we have for the content of any specific Anglo-Saxon meals is the provision for funeral feasts in a fragmentary will from Bury St Edmunds.[9] Here it is envisaged that the meal will be made up of bread, accompanied by bacon and a buck in one case, and in the second by a pig, a bullock and three bucks, in addition to cheese, fish and milk. The relative amounts of money allowed for each of these commodities (assuming that bread was much cheaper than animal foods) suggests that the bulk of the first meal was accounted for by the bread, but in the second the other foods, which are worth about twice as much, must have been more substantial. In other documents, the food to go with bread is called *sufle*.[10] This Old English word is sometimes translated 'relish', but, in the light of the Bury will, it does not seem to me that it should be interpreted as a mere seasoning. No doubt the amount of *sufle*, and probably the food it was made of as well, will have varied with the occasion, and with the social standing of the people eating it. Peasants probably always ate more bread and less *sufle* than aristocrats, and many more of their meals will have involved cereals in some form other than bread.

The importance of bread in Anglo-Saxon life and thought is also indicated by the vocabulary of social relationships: the word 'lord', Old English *hlaford*, is derived from *hlaf*, 'bread', and *weard*, 'keeper, guardian'. The implication is that, in early Anglo-Saxon society, the lord looked after, and provided, bread for his dependants, presumably members of his household. It is unlikely that the lord himself played any part in making the bread, but at his side was the lady, Old English *hlafdige*, or 'bread-kneader'. The rulers of this society were therefore not totally divorced from the production of the food they distributed. Lord and lady were of course vital to the structure of English society in the Anglo-Saxon period and long afterwards, but it was always their dependants who produced the food, and ultimately consumed a good deal of it. A lord's followers are usually referred to simply as his 'men', but there is a rare word, *hlafæta*, 'bread-eater', for a dependant of a *ceorl* (commoner).[11] Although this word only survives in this context, it may well have been used of the dependants of aristocrats as well, and thus the whole of Anglo-Saxon society can be seen in terms of bread-keepers, bread-kneaders, and their bread-eaters.

We need to explain this change in the status of bread since the Anglo-Saxon period, and I would do that in terms of the work involved. For us, bread is a convenience food. It is easier to buy a loaf (or even a ready-made sandwich) than cook potatoes, pasta, or any other cereal. In many cases we don't even have to slice it. For the Anglo-Saxons, the situation was quite different: grinding the flour for bread was a huge amount of labour, before one could even begin to bake it. Mechanical mills only came in around the middle of the Anglo-Saxon period. Before that, all flour had to be ground by hand in a quern. The amount of energy required for this task can only be understood by visiting a museum where it is possible to try out a repro- duction hand quern. My own experiments suggest that the average mod- ern person would not last half an hour at such work, and would have produced enough flour for a couple of rolls. King Æthelberht of Kent had a whole class of female slaves (the middle one of three in terms of status) identified by their task of grinding flour.[12] Since this was such hard work, it was probably carried out by slaves in all establishments that had them, but in most peasant households, grinding will have been the task of the female members of the family. On top of this, women were almost certainly responsible for spinning, weaving and making clothes, milking and caring for domestic animals, dairy work and all food preservation, as well as cook- ing meals and looking after children, so it is understandable if, in a small household, they only ground flour and baked bread occasionally (for how else they cooked their cereals, see below).

Even by the end of the Anglo-Saxon period, when there were over 5,000 mills, mostly watermills, in England, they were not accessible to everyone.[13] Very few of them were in the north or west of England, and where they existed, they were expensive to use. Even for prosperous landlords, a mill was a considerable investment, and to recoup that investment it was expected to make a substantial profit. There is no evidence that anyone was compelled to use their landlord's mill in the Anglo-Saxon period, but presumably, for those who could afford it, paying to have their corn ground would be preferable to doing the work themselves, or having labour tied up when there was other work to be done. On the other hand, there must have been many people for whom the cost of mechanical milling was prohibitive, who, along with those living where there were no commercial mills, still had to do their own grind- ing. Others might have been able to afford milling for special occasions, but will have fallen back on the hand quern, or other ways of preparing cereals, the rest of the time. So bread would not be eaten by everybody at every meal. The richer a household was, the more slaves or servants it included, the more bread it could expect to eat, throughout our period. Bread was therefore a prestigious food, suitable for demonstrating wealth and power, or for feast- ing, if one was less wealthy and powerful.

The main functional advantage of bread is that it keeps well. This means that fuel can be used economically by only making a fire when a fresh

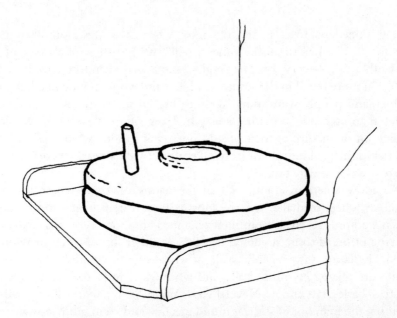

7 *Quern on a wooden stand at Papa Stour, Shetland, 1967. It is unlikely that such stands were in use in Anglo-Saxon England, but the form of the mill does not seem to have changed. The grain was poured into the central hole with one hand, and the top stone turned with the other. The flour came out between the stones and collected on the shelf.* After Fenton, *Northern Isles*

8 *A quern in use, unknown location in the Indian sub-continent, nineteenth century. It is likely that Anglo-Saxon women sat in similar positions to grind their bread-corn.* After W. Simpson, 'Women Grinding Corn'

baking is needed. However, in the winter, when there was more likely to be a fire on the hearth all the time, it will have been less of a luxury to cook other foods every day. The Anglo-Saxons may therefore have baked and eaten more bread in the summer, when a fire would not be needed for heating, and people were more likely to be out in the fields or garden, rather than at home watching the pot. How often they baked would depend on the nature of their bread (in parts of Europe where flat-bread was traditional, baking might only take place twice a year, whereas elsewhere it was a weekly task).

We know a certain amount about the nature of Anglo-Saxon bread. Bread, or wheat to make it, is the most common item in the food rents which landlords received from their tenants. Those food rents that specify the type of bread to be rendered usually ask either for wheaten or white bread. The latter was probably made of wheat too: the words 'wheat' and 'white' are related etymologically, and wheat does in fact make a whiter loaf than barley, rye or oats. Nevertheless, Anglo-Saxon 'white' flour, made by sifting the bran out of stone-ground meal, would seem quite 'brown' to us, used as we are to roller-ground, bleached flour. The preference for wheat over barley is indicated by anecdotes in saints' lives where holy men demonstrate their humility by eating barley bread, and it is also recommended for fasting.[14] Our sources do not tell us about oats or rye as bread-corn, or about mixed cereals. This may mean that they were rarely used, or only that they were not familiar enough to make much impression on the literate classes: for them, the important distinction was between the wheaten bread that they wanted to eat, and the barley bread that many people had to put up with most of the time.

We also have a fair amount of information about how Anglo-Saxon bread was made. That it was normally leavened, not flat-bread, can be inferred from one of the riddles in the tenth-century *Exeter Book of Old English Poetry*:

> *I heard that something grew in a corner,*
> *swelled up and rose, lifting its cover;*
> *a bride grasped the boneless thing*
> *with her proud hands, a lord's daughter*
> *clothed the swelling object with a covering.*[15]

For the double meaning to work here, the proving of dough needs to be as familiar as male sexual arousal. The preference for wheat also indicates leavened bread, since, apart from its colour, the main advantage of wheat over barley is that it rises better, giving a lighter loaf. If people normally made unleavened bread, barley, oats or rye would be just as good, and in fact that is what they may have done in areas where wheat was not grown. Fresh yeast would normally be available as a by-product of brewing (see below), and sour-dough, saved from a previous baking, may also have been in use. One early food rent distinguishes between 'sour' and 'clean' bread, perhaps indicating the two methods of raising dough.[16]

There are also references to both 'hearth-baked' and 'oven-baked' bread, indicating that both methods were familiar.[17] The latter may have been restricted to the upper levels of society, however. Only two written descriptions survive of baking bread in an oven, both in a monastic context.[18] Ovens have been excavated on quite a few Anglo-Saxon sites, and some at least must have been for baking bread, but it is difficult to distinguish these from kilns for drying or parching grain, or for preparing malt.[19] Thus it is hard to estimate what proportion of Anglo-Saxon households had ovens: they may have been common in larger establishments, both lay and ecclesiastical, certainly by the end of the period, but perhaps never common in peasant homes. The type of oven indicated by both archaeology and one of the literary references is the single-chamber type, which historically has been the most common type in most parts of the world.[20] It is a clay dome under which a fire is lit, the door shut up, and then, when it has burnt out, the ashes cleaned out and the bread put in to bake. Bread rises better in an oven than on the hearth-stones, but an oven is quite an investment in both materials and labour. In many parts of the world they have never been standard household equipment; instead there will be one in each village or neighbourhood, either communally owned or operated commercially in much the same way as a mill.[21] However, there is no evidence for such arrangements in Anglo-Saxon England, so it may be that peasant families did not have access to ovens at all.[22] In this case their loaves will have been rather shallowly risen (unless

9 *Barley and wheat loaves, made with the same technique using the same weight of flour, showing relative rising qualities. The barley rises less and, as the sections show, has a denser texture. However, its flavour is preferred in areas where it is traditional.* After Renfrew, *Palaeoethnobotany*

10 *Woman baking bread in an outdoor single-chamber oven, Taos Pueblo, New Mexico, from a postcard of the 1960s. She is taking the loaves out of the oven with a long-handled wooden peel. Attempts to reconstruct such ovens at Bede's World, Jarrow, and West Stow, Suffolk, have shown that they need to be under cover in the British climate, but they must have been used in the same way*

baked under a pot), probably quite small by our standards, and almost certainly round. The sign in the *Monasteriales indicia* for bread is to join the thumbs and forefingers in a circle; if this is an accurate indication of size, as well as shape, the Anglo-Saxon loaf was not much bigger than a modern roll.

Recently, some carbonised loaves have been found in Ipswich, during the excavation of a house that burned down during the eleventh century (see **colour plate 5**).[23] These finds are unique, as British archaeological conditions very rarely preserve prepared food (in contrast to the dry conditions of Egypt, for instance). It is not clear whether these loaves were made before or after the Norman Conquest, but it is unlikely that the change of regime brought about major changes in baking practice. The loaves are round, about 4 inches in diameter, having presumably shrunk in the fire more than they would have in the course of ordinary baking, and are made of mixed wheat and rye.[24] How typical they are of eleventh-century English bread, let alone of earlier parts of the period, is very hard to say: we can only hope for further finds to compare them with. It is interesting, though, to compare their evidence with what we know from other sources: size and shape are confirmed, but the use of mixed grains is quite unknown otherwise. There is evidence from the Continent for larger loaves, but these may have been associated specifically with commercial production.[25] There is a certain amount of Anglo-Saxon evidence for different sizes of bread (large and small), but it is hard to know how much they differed.[26] Only in one case is the size of a loaf specified, and then it is 'as broad as the palm of the hand'.[27] This loaf was to be buried to ensure the fertility of the field, but the evidence of *Monasteriales indicia* and the Ipswich finds suggest that bread for eating was not much bigger.

As well as being made of mixed grains, Anglo-Saxon bread is likely to have contained other admixtures. Early medieval grain-processing technology would not have allowed all weed seeds to be removed from the corn before it was ground; any seeds of a similar size to the grain would contribute towards the finished flour (and indeed the following year's seed-corn). In the case of some weeds, such as wild oats, this might have been regarded as an advantage (the Anglo-Saxons were not concerned with 'sample purity', and a few oat grains would not affect the rising capabilities of the dough). One which might cause problems, however, is the corncockle. This was probably the most serious weed of Anglo-Saxon cornfields.[28] It was so ubiquitous that its name, *coccel*, was used to translate

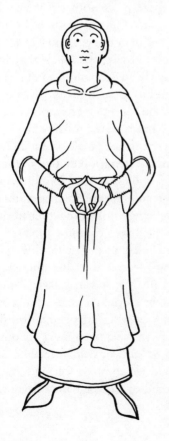

11 Left: *Sign for bread from the* Monasteriales indicia. Author's reconstruction

12 Above right: *Corncockle (*Agrostemma githago) *was a very serious weed of cereals in Anglo-Saxon England and until the introduction of chemical pesticides. The flower is bright purple.* After Keble Martin, *Concise British Flora*

the Vulgate's *lolium*, where the Authorised Version has 'tares'.[29] It may have been regarded with particular horror not so much because it was common, but because its seeds are about the same size as cereal grains, and it is poisonous.[30] Even if no weeds contaminated the meal, however, it is bound to have contained minute pieces of grit from the surface of the millstones. The long-term effect of this was such that many Anglo-Saxons' teeth were so worn by middle age that the dentine was exposed, leaving them in considerable pain and possibly unable to eat.[31]

OTHER CEREAL FOODS

The house where the Ipswich loaves were found does not appear to have been a particularly high-status one. However, Ipswich is one of the oldest trading settlements in England, and by the end of the Anglo-Saxon period town-dwellers were beginning to live a different lifestyle from their rural contemporaries, partly because they were more prosperous. So it may be that these Ipswich citizens belonged to the more affluent section of society, aligning themselves with the aristocracy rather than the peasantry in terms of diet, as well as, quite possibly, other aspects of their lives. But if they had not been able to do this, what might they have been eating instead of bread? As I argued above, although everybody would have eaten bread when they could, it would cost too much, in terms of labour or money, for poorer people to eat it most of the time. Their everyday meals were probably based on what is usually known in modern English as 'pottage'. This is an unfamiliar word because until recently it was an unfamiliar item of diet, but 'one-pot meals' have now begun to come back into fashion. The Old English name for these dishes is *briw*, and there are several recipes for such concoctions in the Anglo-Saxon medical texts. Apart from being cooked together in one pot, the main feature of these dishes is that they were composed mainly of cereals or pulses, other ingredients being included, in the medical recipes, mainly for their healing potential. For non-medical use, the amount of other foods might have been reduced even further, and may have constituted little more than flavouring. The consistency would have been that of a soup or stew, or somewhere in between, or a porridge, depending on the base ingredient. Other ingredients are likely to have been leeks or other vegetables of the onion family, cabbage of some kind, or wild vegetables (see chapter on vegetables) or perhaps salted or dried meat or fish. The traditional easterledge or dock pudding, composed of oats or barley flavoured with wild herbs, is a descendant of this kind of dish.[32]

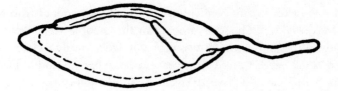

13 *A sprouted grain of barley. The rootlet has emerged from the base, but the shoot remains within the outer skin. Sprouting turns the starch in the grain into sugars (within the pecked line). The grain is then roasted to prevent further growth and create the characteristic malty flavour*

Most cereals (and pulses) take a long time to cook by boiling. As indicated above, this need not have been a problem in the winter, when people may have been indoors anyway, sitting around the fire to keep warm. This kind of cookery does not require constant attention, as long as there is enough liquid in the pot to stop the contents burning. If the fire was lit first thing in the morning, or rekindled if it had been banked up overnight, the food could have been put on to cook then, and been ready to eat by early afternoon. Cooking times could have been accelerated by cracking or crushing the grains (a hand-quern is still used for this in many parts of the world where flour is now ground mechanically) or pre-soaking them in cold water. The flavouring ingredients would need less cooking, and could be added at a later stage, although later medieval recipes suggest that vegetables were usually 'cooked to death' by modern standards.[33]

BEER

The third main cereal product in the Anglo-Saxon diet was beer. To say that beer played an important role in Anglo-Saxon life is not to impugn the character of the ancestral English: it was undoubtedly a significant factor in early medieval nutrition, as the main source of sugars. The only other substantial source was fruit, which would only be available in season. Beer was certainly the most common drink for the Anglo-Saxons; they might have preferred wine and mead, but these were both expensive, for different reasons, and so mainly available to the upper classes. It is generally believed that people did not usually drink water in the Middle Ages, since its safety was unreliable, and milk was only seasonally available. The drink most likely to appear at Anglo-Saxon meals, therefore, or to be drunk between them, was beer. Beer, or the malt to make it, is the next most common item in food rents after bread, confirming that it was a standard feature of the Anglo-Saxon table.[34] This does not mean that people were drunk all the time; most of what they drank was probably what would in later centuries be called 'small beer', a good deal weaker than what we find in pubs today. Even so, people would have derived a considerable proportion of their calories from both the sugars and the alcohol in beer.

The ingredients of Anglo-Saxon beer were fundamentally what they are today: water, malt and hops, or other flavouring herbs, and yeast. There is a reference in a medical recipe to beer based on malted wheat, but this may be for medicinal reasons.[35] Most Anglo-Saxon beer was almost certainly based on barley, and this would account for the large amounts of barley still being grown even when wheat had superseded it for bread-making. Malted barley and oats were found in the same Ipswich house as the loaves already mentioned.[36] Barley has been identified on other archaeological sites which had sprouted before being roasted, and, although both sprouting and roasting could have been accidental, it is likely that at least most of these represent malting for brewing. Malting kilns have also been identified, although, as already mentioned, it is hard to tell these from baking ovens or parching kilns. Malt was also required as part of some food rents, rather than the finished beer, probably because it is easier to store.

It is often stated that hops were not used in brewing in England before the sixteenth century, but they are native to Britain, and it is unlikely that their preservative and flavouring properties went unnoticed. However, there is only a little evidence for their use in brewing in the Anglo-Saxon period. The best known comes from the tenth-century boat found in the Thames estuary at Graveney in Kent.[37] The timbers of the boat were crammed with the fruits of hops, in quantities to indicate that the whole cargo must have consisted of hop-plants at the fruiting stage of development. The only purpose for which fruiting hops are used is brewing; the young shoots can be eaten as a vegetable, but there are no fruits on the plant at that stage. If large amounts of hops were being transported for brewing, their use must have been a standard practice. Indeed, since Kent has more recently been a hop-growing area, it maybe that the Graveney cargo was being shipped to some part of the country where they did not grow so well. Hops have also been found in an Anglo-Saxon deposit in Ipswich.[38] This is not to say that no unhopped ale was brewed in Anglo-Saxon England: bog-myrtle (*Myrica gale*) is required in one of the medicinal brewing recipes,[39] and other herbs may have been used as well. But it seems unlikely that hops were entirely unknown in English brewing before, as the rhyme goes, 'Hops, reformation, bays and beer / Came to England all in one year.'[40]

As far as the yeast is concerned, this would be a top-fermenting strain, forming a 'head' on the brewing vessel and resulting in an ale, rather than a lager, in modern terms. Bottom-fermenting lager yeasts were apparently not exploited before the sixteenth century, and even later in England.[41] Whether the Anglo-Saxons normally saved yeast from one brewing to the next (there would be plenty for both brewing and bread-making) or allowed wild yeasts to colonise the wort, we do not know. The medicinal brew with bog-myrtle uses 'fresh yeast', presumably straight from an active brewing vessel, and this could have been the usual practice where brewing went on more or less continuously. Where the amount of beer consumed did not require continuous production, yeast could have been saved for a short period if it was kept cool.[42]

That Anglo-Saxon beer was not all the same is apparent from other evidence. The food rent in the laws of King Ine of Wessex (?AD 694) asks for two kinds, Welsh (or British, or foreign, or even pertaining to slaves – Old English

14 Right: *Triangular silver-gilt mount from one of the Sutton Hoo drinking horns, showing the elaborate decoration considered appropriate for such vessels.* After Rupert Bruce-Mitford, The *Sutton Hoo Ship Burial: a Handbook*, British Museum 1968

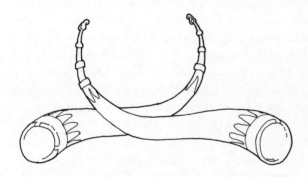

15 Above left: *Pair of drinking horns from the seventh-century burial at Sutton Hoo, Suffolk, almost certainly that of a king of East Anglia. They have been reconstructed as horns of aurochs, the wild ancestor of domestic cattle, since the fittings are too big for cow-horns. This means the horns must have been either imported from the Continent, or brought over by the deceased's ancestors, since aurochs were extinct in Britain before the Anglo-Saxons arrived. Such expenditure, in either money or effort, shows the importance attached to drinking vessels in traditional Anglo-Saxon society.* After Bruce-Mitford, *Sutton Hoo*

wylisc can mean any of these) and clear.[43] A medical recipe also mentions these two kinds, although in this case either is acceptable.[44] The implication seems to be that the Welsh (or slaves, or whoever) drank, or made, cloudy beer, or perhaps most beer was cloudy. It seems likely that the clear type was considered preferable. Other food rents ask for a third type, 'soft', or 'mild' beer, suggesting that the others may have had a tendency to taste rather harsh.[45]

Some beer would no doubt taste harsh, or worse, because something had gone wrong in the brewing. *Bald's Leechbook* has a procedure to prevent this happening, involving the use of lupins which have blessed, perhaps unwittingly, by a priest.[46] 'Sour beer' is mentioned in the medical texts as if this was something normally available.[47] Whether this means just a bit sour, for instance from being left standing in an open jug overnight, or sour enough to be called vinegar, is hard to say. There is an Old English word, *eced*, for 'vinegar', derived from Latin *acetum*; this may have meant wine vinegar rather than malt, or it may have covered vinegar of any origin. In the latter case, 'sour beer' would mean beer that was only slightly sour, but if *eced* means wine vinegar only, malt vinegar would be *sure eala*.[48] Malt vinegar would certainly be more widely available than that from wine, and there may have been a wide variety of uses for beer ranging from not quite fit to drink to real vinegar. Beer and its products would be so ubiquitous that their role in the domestic economy must have been of considerable significance.

The social role of beer in Anglo-Saxon England was undoubtedly important, too. Hugh Magennis has shown how vital drinking was in creating and reinforcing relationships both within and between families, and, especially, between lords and retainers.[49] These relationships were the infrastructure of Anglo-Saxon society, providing people with identity and security both as members of kinship groups and as dependants of powerful men. Drinking together helped the individuals involved get to know each other better, and created obligations between host and guest. Wine and mead would undoubtedly have been the favoured media for such semi-ceremonial drinking, but the vast majority of English drinking sessions, then as now, must have involved beer. Drinking beer together cements many relationships in England at the present day, but these are not the relationships that determine our status in society, our security from violence, our economic stability, or our access to legal justice. What is now merely a recreational activity was undoubtedly that for the Anglo-Saxons too, but it could also be a matter of life or death for them, or at least a matter of the quality of life. Beer, then, was as important as bread or any other form of cereal food in Anglo-Saxon life. Indeed, arguably it was more important, since even bread, the staff of life, did not play the same role in creating an Anglo-Saxon's social persona.

—☙ TWO ❧—

ADDING INTEREST
Vegetables, Herbs and Other Flavourings

The Anglo-Saxon diet was not composed entirely of cereals, despite the impression that may have been given in the previous chapter. There were alternatives, and in times when cereals were in short supply, these must have been of vital importance. Actual famines were rare enough to merit a mention in the *Anglo-Saxon Chronicle*,[1] but relative shortages of corn must have been very common as stores ran low and people waited anxiously for the new crop to ripen. At these times they must have been glad to eat wild plants, as well as the 'pot-herbs' they grew in their gardens, and fortunately both are plentiful in summer as harvest time approaches. In really bad years, people may have collected and eaten beech mast and acorns instead of cereals. At all times, however, there was an alternative to cereals, suitable for pottage if not for bread, that shared many of their advantages, being high in protein as well as carbohydrates, and easy to store, and introduced an element of variety into the diet: the pulses.

PULSES

For the Anglo-Saxons, pulses meant peas and beans; there is no evidence that the other European legumes, lentils and chick-peas, were grown or imported. Before runner and 'French' beans came in from the Americas, beans in Europe meant the Faba bean, *Vicia faba*. This is the species that broad beans (*V. faba* var. *major*) belong to, but they are an improved garden variety that in their present form belong to the early modern period of plant-breeding. The form available in the early Middle Ages was what is now known as the field, horse or tick bean (*V. faba* var. *minor*), now grown, if at all, as animal feed or green manure. This has

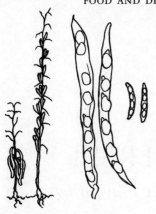

16 *Plants (left) and pods (right) of* Vicia faba, *vars* major *and* minor, *broad and field beans respectively. It can be seen that var.* minor *has more but smaller pods, each containing fewer beans, which are also smaller than those of var.* major. *After Hebblethwaite,* Faba Bean

smaller seeds than broad beans (hence the name of the latter), and fewer of them in a pod, but the plant is taller, bearing more pods, so that the weight of beans per plant may be quite similar.[2] However, the beans have a stronger, earthier flavour than broad beans, and a tougher seed-coat, especially when dried. In later medieval recipes, considerable trouble was taken to remove these 'holes' (hulls), but these recipes catered to the most refined tastes.[3] Even upper-class Anglo-Saxons would probably have been able to cope with bean-skins.

There is some evidence, though, that beans were regarded as rather basic fare, and peas more delicate. These latter are certainly more difficult to grow in the British climate, and thus would involve a greater investment of labour and attention. It is likely that they were grown in gardens rather than in the fields like beans. However, this should not lead us to think that they were the green-seeded garden peas that we grow today. These, again, are a modern development. Anglo-Saxon peas would have been grey, at least when dried, the type now known as field peas, wherever the Anglo-Saxons grew them. The Old English medical texts recommend peas as invalid food, as part of a 'light' diet, which would be unlikely if they were seen as peasant food. Beans, on the other hand, are to be avoided by some sick people,[4] and, according to *Rectitudines singularum personarum*, should be provided for female slaves to eat.[5] It is likely, then, that peas were mainly eaten by the upper classes, who had the necessary labour at their disposal. The existence of a sign for peas, as well as one for beans, in the *Indicia*, suggests that they were expected to be a regular part of monastic diet.[6]

Medical references to 'juicy' peas suggest that they were normally eaten in pottage form, something like the modern 'mushy' peas of chip-shop fame.[7] They are likely to have been cooked with some flavourings, however, if they were the main dish of a meal, rather than a mere accompaniment. Dependent on the amount of water they were cooked in, and the length of cooking time, the consistency could have been anything from separate peas in water or stock, to solid pease pudding (for recipes, see Chapter 6). Most peas would have been cooked from dried, exploiting their keeping qualities in the winter when few fresh vegetables were available, but fresh ones may have been cooked in similar ways in their season. Beans were no doubt cooked by the same methods as peas, perhaps less delicately flavoured as a coarser food. They may also have been used in bread when cereals were in short supply, although always mixed with as much corn as possible, as bread made entirely of beans would be completely flat, extremely heavy and seriously indigestible, as they have no elastic protein to hold air bubbles. Only people facing starvation would willingly eat such bread.

LEEKS AND THEIR RELATIVES

Traditionally, it has been well known on the continent of Europe that 'The English only know three vegetables, and two of those are cabbage.' This was not true in the early Middle Ages, however; at that time, at least two of them would have been leeks. Leeks are now associated with the Welsh, rather than the English, but this probably goes back to a time when the Welsh remained loyal to medieval eating patterns, while the English had begun to expand their repertoire of vegetables.[8] This time lay far in the future in the Anglo-Saxon period, however; for them, a vegetable garden was a *leactun*, a 'leek-enclosure'.[9] This did not mean that only leeks were grown in it, merely that they were the most important of its crops, like the kale in the later Scottish kail-yard.[10] Nor was the leek the only *leac*, confusingly; the onion was *ynneleac* (the first element from Latin *unio*, which also gives us 'onion'), garlic was *garleac* ('spear-leek', after the shape of the leaves) and several others of its relations were known by similar compound names. Any or all of these might be grown in the *leactun*, but the leek, after which all others were named, was clearly the most important.[11]

The enormous popularity of the leek with the Anglo-Saxons probably rested on two things: the strength of its flavour, and its hardiness. The *Indicia* sign for leeks (the only vegetable apart from the pulses with their own sign) requires one to 'put your hand to your nose as if you were smelling something'.[12] When vegetables were normally cooked in pottage with bland cereals or pulses, delicacy of flavour only meant that more had to be picked, washed and chopped. It was only when plain boiled vegetables superseded all-in-one cooking that individual savours began to be appreciated. For the Anglo-Saxons, then, leeks, onions and garlic had one distinct advantage, in that a little went a long way. Another was that they were available through the winter, leeks in the garden, and onions and garlic in store. Later in the Middle Ages, leeks were especially associated with Lent, when it would be unacceptable to put bacon, or a bone, in the pot to improve the flavour of pottage, and this may have been true in the Anglo-Saxon period too. There is little evidence that the Anglo-Saxons stored vegetables in general through the winter, but there is a touching story of St Cuthbert, shortly before his death at his hermitage on Farne Island, subsisting on a few onions.[13] As the saint died in March, these cannot have been fresh onions, especially on that exposed site, so they must have been dried and stored through the winter. There is no similar anecdote about garlic, but as they are preserved in exactly the same, very simple, way, it is likely that they had a similar role in the Anglo-Saxon diet.

What we know of the role of onions and garlic in Anglo-Saxon thought (as opposed to real life) is based on three riddles from the collection in the tenth-century *Exeter Book of Old English Poetry*. Two of these, 'A one-eyed garlic seller' and one on the onion that states 'I don't bite anyone unless they bite me', clearly draw on the relatively learned late antique tradition of Latin *enigmata*, but the 'earthy' character of the other onion riddle has led to it being classified as rather more popular culture:

I am a wonderful creature,   a joy among women,
necessary to the neighbours;   I harm none
of the townspeople   except my destroyer alone.
My stalk is tall,   I stand in a bed,
rough somewhere underneath.   Sometimes
a very beautiful   daughter of a man,
a proud-hearted girl,   dares to take hold of me,
rushes me when I'm red,   grabs my head,
fixes me in a safe place.   At once she feels
her meeting with me,   she who confines me,
the curly-haired woman;   wet is her eye.[14]

Although it is the ambiguity of this riddle that has usually drawn the attention of scholars, it does also tell us something about what the Anglo-Saxons expected an onion to look (and taste) like: a tall stalk, red colouring and a 'head', presumably a bulb, as well as eye-watering qualities, were all familiar enough to contribute to the double meaning.

CABBAGES AND OTHER BRASSICAS

The Alliums were clearly the most significant vegetables in the Anglo-Saxon diet, but, although cabbage was not number-one vegetable as it is now, the brassicas were probably next in importance. In *Bald's Leechbook*, leeks and cabbage (*por* and *cawel*) are linked as foods that are hard to digest and therefore unsuitable for certain patients.[15] The variety of cabbage grown was probably close to the wild type, which may be native to parts of the British Isles,[16] or to kale or spring greens. Heading varieties of cabbage had almost certainly been developed by the Romans,[17] but there is no evidence that they were known in Anglo-Saxon England. Some varieties do seem to be known: there are references to a 'broad cabbage' and to red cabbage,[18] but the selection of this colour variant need not imply anything like the hard, dense red cabbages of today. Wild cabbage is now thought almost inedible because of its strong taste, and the length of time it takes to cook,[19] but these characteristics would be no disadvantage if it was used to flavour a slow-cooking pottage, as it was much more recently in Scotland.[20] In such cookery there would be no demand either for delicate flavours or for such curiosities as cauliflower or Brussels sprouts, which in any case seem to be modern developments.[21]

Archaeologically, cabbage seeds (*Brassica oleracea*) are hard to distinguish from those of other brassicas, and even from other members of the Cruciferae, so we depend mainly on written sources, especially the medical texts, for specific evidence for vegetables in this group. Cabbages appear most often by far, but turnips also occur. Old English *næp* is the ancestor of modern English 'turnip' (although Scots 'neep' is closer to the original form), and must refer to the same vegetable. But there does seem to be confusion in the glossary entries between Latin *napus*, 'turnip', (from which *næp* is derived) and *rapa*, 'rape'.[22] In fact the confusion persisted to the extent that the botanical name of the turnip was until recently *Brassica rapa* (now *B. campestris*), and rape is *B. napus*.[23] Perhaps *næp* was borrowed when the meanings of the Latin words were changing. If these two vegetables were hard to tell apart, it cannot have been because turnips look like the 'rape-turnip' or swede (also a form of B. *napus*); these were not introduced into England until the eighteenth century.

However, the existence of so many different forms of rape (oil-seed rape, swede, and forms grown for their leaves for animal feed) and turnip (our type is derived from a form grown for oilseed, and some far-eastern 'cabbages' also belong to *B. campestris*) shows that both species are highly variable. The forms of both vegetable familiar to the Anglo-Saxons are likely to have been close to the wild species, with none of these characteristics especially prominent. They may have used leaves, seeds (perhaps for seasoning, since there is no evidence they had oil-extraction technology) and roots, as and when they were available. The leaves may have been most valuable in the spring, as both species are usually biennial, and thus sprout early. Seed would be ready in the second summer, but would store well, while the roots would be at their best at the end of the first summer, ready to feed the plant through the winter. However, these roots would not be anything like the size of modern varieties, which are the product of deliberate breeding, and there is no evidence that their storage potential was exploited by the Anglo-Saxons. In fact the only roots we know for sure were kept through the winter are St Cuthbert's onions (see previous section).

OTHER ROOTS

As with turnip and rape, there is no evidence that the Anglo-Saxons stored carrots, parsnips or beets over the winter. None of them would have such impressive roots as they do today, and all these plants may in fact have been grown for their leaves. Ford-Lloyd believes the 'Roman red beet' with its fleshy root was not introduced into England until the sixteenth century,[24] and the Anglo-Saxon evidence does not contradict this: there is no mention of red colour, and although the roots of beet are mentioned, other parts of the plant occur too.[25] As the 'sea-beet' is native to England,[26] it may be this that is referred to: one recipe asks for 'the beets that grow everywhere'.[27] Some of these may have been of a reddish colour, which appears as a natural variation in wild plants, while others might be darker or lighter green, or even yellowish. All these variants can be seen today in sugar-beet, spinach-beet and chard, as well as beetroot, all of which belong to the same species, *Beta vulgaris*.[28]

All the same uncertainties apply to carrots (*Daucus carota*) and parsnips (*Pastinaca sativa*), along with an extra one, also concerned with colour. It seems that there was considerable confusion between parsnips and carrots throughout antiquity and the Middle Ages. Latin *pastinaca* meant 'parsnip', but could also be applied to carrots. In Old English they were both called *more*, but this seems also to mean any other fleshy root. Some subtypes of *more* were distinguished, the most frequent being *feldmore*, '*more* of open country', i.e. wild, and *wealhmore*, probably 'foreign *more*'.[29] The former probably means the native carrot, and the latter the parsnip, but even that is not certain. How could such confusion arise? Surely carrots and parsnips are completely different?

Or perhaps they were not so different in the past. For one thing, it is unlikely that any cultivated carrot was known in Europe before the thirteenth century.[30] The Anglo-Saxon (and classical) carrot would therefore be the native wild one, with an undeveloped, woody root of a dirty whitish colour.[31] The orange carrot we know today was not bred until the seventeenth century, being preceded by purple and then yellow types.[32] All these colours, at least in less intense versions, occur as natural variations, and it is evidently easy to manipulate the pigmentation of carrots. All this work, however, lay in the future in the early Middle Ages. Meanwhile, what was the parsnip like? The wild form has a tough, dry root, whitish in colour like the cultivated form.[33] From this point of view the two roots might be thought fairly similar, but the parsnip would be bigger than the carrot, and the above-ground parts of the plants would be hard to confuse.[34] However, there is better evidence for Roman cultivation and selection of parsnips than carrots, and it may be that the parsnip was more familiar to classical authors, who regarded the carrot as a less important version of the same thing.[35] At the present day, the parsnip is a completely unimportant crop compared to the carrot, and so much less research has been devoted to it. Authorities even differ over whether it is native to the British Isles.[36] It may be then that the wild parsnip was introduced into England, most likely by the Romans, but not yet regarded as part of the English flora by the Anglo-Saxons, or perhaps it was the cultivated form that was introduced, but not yet very different from the wild plant. Either situation would allow the Anglo-Saxons to see the parsnip as a 'foreign root'.

Whatever it means, *more* occurs quite frequently in the medical texts, but the only prescription that looks like food, rather than medicine, is one listing warming substances recommended for hiccups caused by cold: 'broth of mint or carrot/parsnip (*more*) or cumin or ginger'.[37] None of the other plants listed is normally valued for its roots, so it may be that above-ground parts, leaves or seeds, are being used as flavouring here.

One root that is definitely a root is the radish, *Raphanus sativus*, since that is what its name, from Latin *radix*, means. In Old English this appears as *rædic*, which translates both *radix* and *raphanum* (root and radish – unless *radix* meant radish too by this stage).[38] Wild radish species are widely distributed, and domestication took place in the Mediterranean region (as well as in the Far East).[39] The single reference in *Bald's Leechbook* to 'southern radish' therefore probably means the cultivated form.[40] Other *rædic* references in medical texts could equally indicate the native *R. maritimum*, which also has a 'stout tap-root', and may have been regarded as a wild variety of the same plant.[41] The patient is usually instructed to eat the radish, sometimes with salt,[42] rather than make it into a potion, but it is still hard to know whether this was something healthy Anglo-Saxons did too.

OTHER LEAVES

As we have seen above, some of the plants we think of as root vegetables may have been used just as much for their leaves. Others, which do not have tap-roots, can only have been valued for this latter part. The Old English *cærse* gives us modern English 'cress' and must have stood for the same kind of plant.

Several types were distinguished, including *tuncærse*, 'town-' or 'garden-cress', evidently a cultivated plant, and *broc cersan*, *wyllecærsan* and *fencersan*, all probably water-cress, *Nasturtium officinale*, or one of its aquatic relatives.[43] *Cærsan wylle* (cress spring) and similar terms occur several times in charters,[44] no doubt indicating places where these native cresses grew wild,[45] and perhaps where people were accustomed to pick them. Whether they picked them to eat cannot be established for certain, as all the references are to medical uses, if they are not mere glosses, but it seems unlikely that such tasty plants would be neglected.

Lettuce, on the other hand, although it has an Old English name, *leahtric*, probably was not eaten by the Anglo-Saxons, as Abbot Ælfric felt the need to explain in a homily for Easter that 'The plant they had to eat with the unleavened bread is called lettuce. It is bitter to eat.'[46] Celery, *merce*, must have been cultivated, since there are quite frequent references to *wudumerce*, 'wild (literally 'wood') celery'.[47] But all these references come from medical texts, and so neither the wild nor cultivated form may have been eaten as food. One wild plant that may have been eaten is *melde*, an Old English term covering the *Chenopodium* species such as Good King Henry and the native fat hen, and perhaps other plants like them, with mealy leaves. Although their leaves are fairly small compared with cultivated vegetables, the plants grow quite big enough to be worth pulling up to eat.[48] It is believe to have been eaten regularly until spinach was introduced in the later Middle Ages.[49] Large numbers of *Chenopodium* seeds on archaeological sites may not mean these plants were eaten, since they could have been growing as weeds, but the number of place names incorporating *melde* (e.g. Melbourn, Cambridgeshire) suggests that people took a particular interest in them.[50]

17 *Fat hen (left) and Good King Henry* (Chenopodium album *and* C. bonus-henricus). *Although* C. bonus-henricus *is considered better eating, and has been used as a vegetable for a very long time, it may not have been introduced into the British Isles until later than our period. The native* C. album, *with its obviously mealy leaves, is more likely to have been the Anglo-Saxon* melde. After B.E. Nicholson, The Oxford Book of Food Plants, 1969 *and Keble Martin,* Concise British Flora

HERBS

The distinction between herbs and vegetables is not one that would have been meaningful to the Anglo-Saxons. As already discussed, they are unlikely to have eaten any vegetable (apart from the pulses) as a dish in itself.[51] A cabbage whose main function was to add flavour to a *briw* would not need to be classified differently from mint doing the same thing. All would be covered by the word *wyrt*, 'plant, vegetable, herb', which survived as 'wort' until the seventeenth century. For our purposes, however, I shall count as 'herbs' those plants so used since the Anglo-Saxon period, and those likely to have been used in smaller quantities than the 'vegetables' discussed above. I shall also confine this section to those flavouring plants that can be used fresh, the leaves and stalks being the parts usually exploited. Those whose parts, particularly seeds and roots, normally appear in dried form, and thus enter into long-distance trade, are dealt with under 'spices' below.

Some of the plants discussed above might be better dealt with here: lettuce, for instance, was equated with the 'bitter herbs' of the Passover, and celery was used in small quantities for flavouring until the blanching varieties were developed in the modern period.[52] Celery seeds are also used as flavouring, and there are numerous references to them in the Anglo-Saxon medical texts, but as they are well known for their diuretic effect, this may not mean they were eaten as food in early medieval England.[53]

In fact most of the familiar culinary herbs were probably associated more with medicine than food in Anglo-Saxon England. It is impossible to make an absolute distinction between the two, as some medical recipes, as we have seen, are for foods rather than potions or poultices, and since most sick people were cared for at home by their relatives, food and medicine must have been prepared by the same people, on the same fire, using the same utensils. Nevertheless, it is in the medical texts that we find extensive references to parsley, sage, thyme, and so on, and very few of them referring to invalid diet rather than strictly medicinal preparations. Dill, for instance, is found in one recipe for a *briw*, and numerous others called *drenc*, drink or potion.[54] Even the *briw* is made entirely of medicinal herbs, but it is described as *mete*, food. Nevertheless, there is no reference to dill in food outside the medical texts, so it seems as if its medicinal properties were valued, rather than its flavour. There are a few archaeological records of dill seeds (*Anethum graveolens*), which must represent human exploitation of some kind, since dill is not a native plant.[55] However, the evidence discussed above makes it more likely that this was for medicinal use than culinary. The status of fennel (*Foeniculum vulgare*) is similar: it appears in numerous medical recipes, only one of them possibly relating to food (a broth) rather than medicine.[56] Its archaeological remains are rare, especially in view of the fact that it may be native to the south of England.[57] However, the fact that its Old English name, *finol*, is derived from Latin, may mean that the Anglo-Saxons did not use the wild plant. *Dile*, on the other hand, is a Germanic word, but if this means that the Anglo-Saxons were already familiar with dill before they arrived in Britain, this is not reflected in the surviving evidence.

Mint (*Mentha* species) is one of the most common herbs in the medical texts.[58] Several types are distinguished (wild, cultivated, fen, brook, white-flowered, and so on), some of them possibly native ones, but again the name comes from Latin. The only recipe that looks like food is the broth mentioned under carrot/parsnip, above, where mint is another of the alternative flavours.[59] Other herbs are much less common, but marjoram, chervil, parsley, sage, possibly thyme, costmary and lovage do occur.[60] Some of the terminology is confused (and nearly all of it Latin in origin), and none of these plants is attested in archaeology, suggesting that none of them was familiar to the Anglo-Saxons. If they were grown, it may only have been in the gardens of the upper classes, and probably for medicinal purposes.

There is not much evidence that herbs were preserved for use out of season, but one recipe does ask for *drige mintan* (dry mint).[61] Another refers to *grene mintan* (probably fresh mint).[62] Such references are rare, however, so it is unlikely that the difference mattered much.

SPICES

Some of the herbs discussed above may have been imported in dry form, especially the ones whose seeds were used. Overseas trade of some kind continued right through the early Middle Ages, with spices and/or drugs (Latin *pigmenta*) one of its low-bulk, high-value mainstays. The merchant in Abbot Ælfric's *Colloquy* lists *pigmenta* among his wares after 'Purple, silk, precious gems and gold, different coloured garments' – all luxury goods.[63]

The most important of the spices was pepper. This was being imported overland from India to the Mediterranean in the Roman period,[64] and reached Britain at that time.[65] It was certainly in England in the eighth century, for it was one of the treasures the Venerable Bede gave away on his deathbed, and Lull (the disciple of Saint Boniface) sent some with a letter home to England from Germany.[66] In the eleventh century, pepper was evidently in use in monastic refectories, for the *Indicia* has a sign for it: 'When you want pepper, knock with one forefinger on the other.'[67] This may mimic grinding, but it is not clear by what means. A *piporcwyrna*, 'pepper-mill', is mentioned in a medical

recipe, but it is not described.[68] In any case, this may have been specialist phar-
maceutical equipment. A *piperhorn* is one of the vessels the prudent reeve was
required to have at his disposal. All these references come from the top end of
Anglo-Saxon society, which is not surprising, since this was also the literate
end, but it may be that in the case of this luxury commodity, the picture is not
distorted by the sources, and pepper really was restricted to the wealthy.

The *piporcwyrna* mentioned above was used to grind not pepper, but cabbage seed, showing that pepper was regarded as the archetypal spice. Others
mentioned in the medical texts are cumin, used to flavour a warming broth, as
we have already seen, but otherwise in straight medicinal preparations, corian-
der, bay berries (and once a bayleaf), ginger and cinnamon.[69] None of these
appear many times, however, and it is likely that their use was largely confined
to medicine. The exception may be something that was probably called a *wyrt-
drenc* – the manuscript of the *Indicia* is corrupt at this point, but the word also
appears in a medical context.[70] The sign for this involves moving one's fist as if
to *wyrta cnocian*, either 'crush herbs' or, as I now think more likely, 'grind
spices'.[71] This may be the *piporcwyrna* again. The Latin equivalent of this sign is
for *potio pigmentata*.[72] What we are not told, however, is which spices went into
these drinks.

Some of the plants discussed earlier in this chapter may have been imported
in dry form, and may therefore be better classified under spices, for example
the seeds of dill, fennel and celery. One spice that was almost certainly grown
here, conversely, is mustard (*Sinapis alba, Brassica nigra*), so classified both
because of its hot taste, and because it is its dried seeds that are normally
used.[73] However, it does not seem to have been especially popular: there are a
few archaeological finds (no doubt there would be more if cruciferous seeds
were easier to tell apart) and a small number of medical recipes, but no evidence that it was used to season food, despite its great popularity later in the
Middle Ages.[74] It does not seem to have been available at monastic tables, as
there is no sign for mustard in the *Indicia*.

SALT

If vegetables, herbs and spices form a continuum, there is a clear distinction
between these and the one mineral item in the Anglo-Saxon diet, salt.
Common salt, sodium chloride, is an essential element in human nutrition
and, probably for that reason, people like it.[75] It is not available everywhere and
so, from the beginnings of human society, some people must have had to
acquire it from a considerable distance. The mechanisms by which this was

achieved in prehistory cannot be known for sure, but in Anglo-Saxon England it was largely distributed by means of trade, although rents and tolls helped supply the more powerful members of society.[76] From the Roman period, salt was produced not only along the coast but inland at salt springs such as Droitwich (Worcestershire) and Nantwich (Cheshire).[77] Both inland and coastal production continued during the Anglo-Saxon period (probably without a break, but this cannot be demonstrated).[78] Salt processing sites were valuable, frequently changing hands in their own right, rather than as mere adjuncts to estates, and attracting the attention of the wealthiest landowners.[79]

Salt was important in the Anglo-Saxon diet both for flavouring and preservation. The salter in Abbot Ælfric's *Colloquy* draws attention to both functions when he asks 'Which people enjoy sweet foods without the flavour of salt? Who fills his cellar or store-room without my craft? Look, all your butter and cheese would be lost if I wasn't here to take care of it; you don't even use your vegetables without me.'[80] He does not say what the cellars and store-rooms are filled with, but presumably both pork products and fish would play a part here. Both are discussed in the relevant chapters below.

Salt in cooking and as a condiment appears occasionally in the medical texts, and presumably both practices were standard.[81] Its presence on monastic tables is attested by the *Indicia* sign: 'When you want salt, then shake your hand with your three fingers together, as if you were salting something.'[82] The value attached to salt production sites must mean that the product was highly valued too, but we have no evidence for the Anglo-Saxon period for such practices as seating 'above and below the salt' according to status, nor of elaborate containers for salt.[83] Such practices of course allowed those who could afford it to display their access to salt, in contrast to the many who could not afford it. Since the economy expanded during the Middle Ages, there must have been more 'have-nots' with regard to salt in Anglo-Saxon

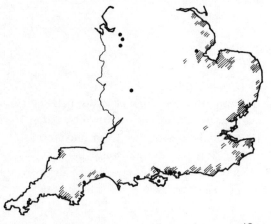

18 *Salt production in Anglo-Saxon England. Dots represent pre-Conquest evidence, shading shows Domesday saltings, which are not likely to be entirely new sites.* After David Hill, *An Atlas of Anglo-Saxon England*, Blackwell 1981

England than later. Nevertheless, salt must have been one of the things that even the poorest had to buy in (the other being iron, or things made of it), however self-sufficient they were in everything else. The word 'buy' of course need not imply that actual coinage changed hands; even by the end of the period, the peasantry were not part of the money economy, except for the odd few who sold their surplus produce in towns. It must have been this surplus, however exiguous, that paid for what salt they could afford, usually by barter of some kind.

HONEY

Honey was of course the only form of sweetening available to the Anglo-Saxons, who no doubt had as sweet a tooth as any other group of people.[84] However, there is little evidence that they used it to sweeten other foods, as we use sugar today. That it sometimes appeared on the table is shown by the existence of a sign in the *Indicia*, and the fact that it is listed next to the sign for salt suggests that it was thought of as a flavouring.[85] There are two recipes in *Bald's Leechbook* for pea soup (?) with honey, but this seems to be an isolated occurrence;[86] recipes for fruit dishes or cakes flavoured with honey are not found. Herbal potions are also sweetened with honey,[87] and these may have been drunk for enjoyment as well as for therapeutic reasons, but sweet foods may have been confined to those with natural sugars (see chapter on fruit).

Honey appears frequently in food rents, showing that the land-owning classes considered it a desirable part of their lifestyle.[88] How the honey required was actually produced is not specified; by the end of the period there is good evidence for bee-keeping, and wild honey may still have been col-

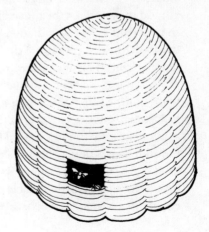

19 *Basketwork skeps like this were undoubtedly the main type of hive in which Anglo-Saxon bees were kept.* Author

lected too. For that matter, bees may have been domesticated from an early stage, given the value placed on their product, but evidence is lacking before the eleventh century. Beehives and bee-keepers are listed in Domesday Book,[89] and there is a bee-keeper (who may either be a slave or have a 'rent-hive') in the *Rectitudines singularum personarum*. If he has a rent-hive, he pays five sesters of honey to the lord, and in some places the *geburs* (the most heavily burdened group of peasants) pay some of their rent in honey too.[90]

In one of the food rents, honey is an alternative to wine, and there are several possible reasons for this.[91] First of all, both products were highly valued; secondly, both may have been sweet – such evidence as there is suggests that in antiquity and the Middle Ages people liked their wine sweet, not being sated with sweet things as we are – and thirdly both were, or could be, alcoholic. Although its value as a sweet food was undoubtedly appreciated, the potential for honey to be turned into mead was probably valued even more. The association of mead with feasting is made clear by the number of compound words based on it, for instance in *Beowulf*.[92] There are of course equivalent compounds based on words for beer and wine, but that only serves to emphasise the importance attached to alcoholic drinks by the Anglo-Saxons. The actual food consumed at feasts is rarely mentioned, and certainly does not contribute in the same way to the sense of occasion. Clearly this literary picture does not simply 'reflect' real life in a straightforward way, but the relative importance of food and drink in heroic verse must have found favour with the patrons of that verse, the Anglo-Saxon aristocracy. It seems to me that these lords would not have allowed their honey to have been consumed as food, except in very small quantities, if it could have been turned into mead.

The particular importance of mead in Anglo-Saxon England is suggested by a miracle story in a late saint's life, Wulfstan of Winchester's *Vita* of Bishop Æthelwold. This story, of King Eadred visiting Æthelwold's monastery at Abingdon, seems to be based on that of the marriage feast at Cana, but here it is mead that provides the miraculous draught: 'The king ... ordered the guests to be served with lavish draughts of mead ... the servants drew off drink all day to the heart's content of the diners, but the level in the containers could not be reduced below a palm's measure.'[93] The difference may be simply that this was a real incident, in which the king happened to order mead and not wine. On the other hand, even if the story is in fact true, wine may still have had exotic associations for the English, or its use in the liturgy may have made it unsuitable. As the story is told partly to denigrate the drinking habits of Northumbrians, it may be that a more traditional, but nevertheless high-status drink suited the hagiographer's purposes better. For similar reasons, mead may have been a particularly suitable drink for lords and kings to drink each others' health and reinforce their relationships in real life, too.

THREE

SUMMER'S BOUNTY

Fruit, Fruit Drinks and Nuts

The Anglo-Saxon sweet tooth, largely hypothetical but nevertheless significant, has already been mentioned in the previous chapter. If foods with added sweetening were not part of their diet, people will have especially appreciated foods that are naturally sweet. The two we have met already are in fact, at least in the form they were normally consumed, drinks. Even before it is turned into mead, honey is fairly liquid, so the only solid sweet food available to the Anglo-Saxons would have been fruit. As such, there is no doubt that fruit was regarded as a treat, in much the same way as we still see sweet foods as comforting, self-indulgent and so on, even now we have so many available. The desirability of fruit can only have been increased by its limited availability, both in terms of the finite productivity of trees and bushes (not to mention the difficulty of cultivating some of them), and of seasonality. Only the hard fruits, apples and pears, can be stored (in the absence of sugar, sterilisation or freezing equipment), so most fruits would only be available for a short time each year – shorter than now, for plant breeders have been working on extending their seasons practically ever since.

Many of the fruits we eat today would have been available to the Anglo-Saxons: apples, pears, plums, cherries, strawberries, raspberries, blackberries, gooseberries, and blackcurrants are all native to the British Isles, or at least their wild ancestors are.[1] That means that the Anglo-Saxons could have eaten them, but not necessarily that they did. We cannot assume that what is attractive to us was equally attractive to the Anglo-Saxons. Nor does it help us to decide whether they cultivated these fruits, or collected them from the wild, but this can be an important point, since selection and breeding has altered most fruits drastically. Wild ones are often tiny compared with their domesticated descendants, and may not taste discernibly sweet.

APPLES

Apples, for instance, were domesticated in the Middle East, and cultivated varieties almost certainly introduced into Britain by the Romans.[2] Cultivated apples were certainly known in Anglo-Saxon England, as we have references to both wild, or sour, apples and sweet ones, and even to *manigfeald æppelcyn*, 'various kinds of apples'.[3] At the end of the eighth century, Charlemagne's *Capitulare de uillis* lists nine apple varieties, including earlies, keepers, and ones for eating straight away, but in England there is no evidence that such fine distinctions were made.[4] One apple variety currently in cultivation in England, Decio, is said to be of Roman origin (see **colour plate 11**).[5] There is no evidence that it was introduced to Britain, but this small, fresh-tasting variety is more likely to resemble the apples grown in Anglo-Saxon England than the known medieval varieties, none of which is recorded before the twelfth century.[6] These latter, nearly all with French names, probably represent a renewed interest in selection and breeding after our period.

The cultivation of apples requires a relatively sophisticated level of horticultural technology. Wild and domesticated types readily interbreed, so seedling trees may 'revert'. To maintain their desirable qualities, cultivated varieties have to be grafted. This technique is mentioned as a 'spring' task (February to April) in the *Gerefa*, a list of the duties of stewards of large estates.[7] It may therefore have been only the upper classes who benefited from grafted apple trees, free from contamination by native crabs. The only extensive Anglo-Saxon references to orchards come from Ælfric Bata's *Colloquies*, where the boys of the monastic school are grilled about whether they have been in the *pomerium*, and with whose permission, and later about which of them stole apples and hid them in their rooms.[8] Although we have no references to orchards forming part of secular aristocratic estates, it is very likely that they did. The word *æppeltun* ('apple-enclosure') occurs reasonably frequently, usually translating *pomerium*, and has given rise to numerous place names.[9] Although in place names it may in fact mean 'apple-village', as a word in everyday speech its most natural translation must be 'orchard'. Anglo-Saxon orchards may not all have been dedicated solely to the growing of apples, but these are likely to have been the most common cultivated fruit. They share with pears the great advantage of keeping into the winter, when no fresh fruit is available, and in the British climate are much easier to grow.

In the hedgerows and woods near orchards there must have been many seedlings from cultivated trees, and hybrids between these varieties and crabs, so the population at large may have had access to sweet apples of some kind. It has been suggested that fruit trees may have been planted deliberately in hedges and odd pockets of waste, and this would certainly be an economical use of land for those with limited areas at their disposal.[10] Such practices would result in a wide variety of crab and cultivated apples, with many intermediate types, being found apparently wild in the countryside, and would account for such expressions as 'wood sour apples', ones that were not only growing in the woods but were also genuine crabs.[11] Apples of whatever type may have been more common in the south of England than in the north, however. At the present day, crab-apples are uncommon in Scotland, and so they may be at the edge of their native range there and in northern England. This would provide an explanation for the distribution of *æppel-* place names, which are particularly common in North Yorkshire. It may be that, in parts of the country where apples were a common sight, both wild and in cultivation, they were not distinctive enough to name settlements after, but where they were rare, the places where they grew might be remarked upon in this way.

PEARS

The British distribution of pears is even more restricted; they may only be native in Devon and Cornwall, and the cultivated pear is of a different species to these.[12] The distribution of 'pear' place names is much more southerly, suggesting that pear-trees were remarkable anywhere in England, and probably absent in the north. The fact that the English word 'pear' is derived from Latin *pyrus* may suggest that the English did not take much notice of the wild plant, either in England or in their continental homelands (if it grew there), or may not have associated the cultivated fruit with the wild one. The wild pear certainly has very small, hard fruits, even less attractive than crab-apples. As with apples, the pear was domesticated in the Middle East,[13] and it is likely that the Romans first introduced cultivated varieties to Britain, but whether any of these persisted until the Anglo-Saxon period is impossible to tell. Pears feature much less frequently both in Anglo-Saxon texts and in archaeology than do apples, and it is likely that they had a much less important role in the diet. However, there is a sign for them in the *Monasteriales indicia*, showing that there was at least a need to refer to them in late Anglo-Saxon Benedictine refectories.[14] If monks were eating them, its is likely that the rest of the upper classes were too, but they may not have been so familiar further down the social scale.

PLUMS AND CHERRIES

The origins of the domestic plum are complex, but it is likely that the damson (*Prunus insititia*) arose first, in western Asia, and is one of the ancestors, with *P. cerasifera*, the cherry-plum, and *P. spinosa*, the sloe, of *P. domestica*, the plum, which arose in Europe.[15] Since Old English has separate names, *plyme* and *sla*, for plum and sloe, it is clear that cultivated plums of some kind were known to the Anglo-Saxons, and there is archaeological evidence for both damson and plum, as well as sloe. However, references in Anglo-Saxon literature, and even medical texts, are rare, and it is likely that plums were something of a luxury in early medieval England.[16] They do have a sign in the *Indicia*, and Abbot Ælfric uses them in his *Grammar*, with apples and pears, to demonstrate the relationship between the names of fruits and the trees they grow on in Latin.[17] It may be that plums grew alongside apples and pears in monastic orchards, and were eaten in monastic refectories, but were a rarity elsewhere in Anglo-Saxon England.

The evidence for cherries, even from archaeology, is even thinner than for plums, but the presence of a sign for them in the *Indicia*, together with the fact that the archaeological finds, although referred to *Prunus avium*, the wild cherry, all come from towns, rather than the rural areas where the trees would be growing, does suggest that cherries were eaten in Anglo-Saxon England.[18] However, the only evidence that they were cultivated is the derivation of Old English *cirs* from Latin *cerasum*; if we do not accept the argument that this foreign name must have been introduced along with foreign, improved, varieties of the actual fruit, there is no reason to

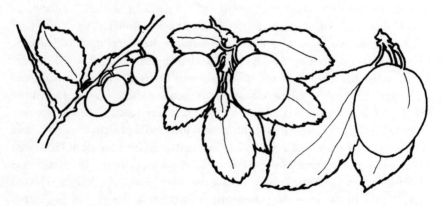

20 *Sloe, bullace and modern domestic plum* (Prunus spinosa, insititia *and* domestica, *respectively*), *to scale*. After Nicholson, *Oxford Book of Food Plants*

think that the domestic *P. cerasus* was introduced into England until after our period. In that case, the cherries in the *Indicia* must have been wild ones, which is quite possible, as the fruits of *P. avium*, although small, are fleshy and often sweet.[19]

BERRIES

The wild strawberry, *Fragaria vesca*, is native to this country, and this is the only type that would have been available to the Anglo-Saxons, since the cultivated strawberry, *F. ananassa*, is derived from American species, and the hautbois strawberry, *F. moschata*, is unlikely to have been introduced this early. Improved strains of the wild species may have been selected, but there is no evidence of this. It is not even certain that they were cultivated, but this does seem likely. All the archaeological remains come from towns, where this low-growing herb is unlikely to have survived unless it was being grown in a protected environment, i.e. a garden. On the other hand, it is equally likely that they were gathered from the wild.[20] There are, remarkably, no references to the fruit in Anglo-Saxon texts, but the plants are mentioned in medical texts.[21] The name for these, *streawberigean wisan*, being based on that of the fruit, is our only evidence that this was the most important part of the plant for the Anglo-Saxons.

Raspberries and blackberries, *Rubus idaeus* and *R. fruticosus* sensu lato, are also found almost exclusively on urban sites, and sometimes in such large numbers that they are unlikely to have been dropped accidentally.[22] In fact, the most likely explanation for these large deposits is that they had passed through the human gut, but there is no real evidence as to whether they were cultivated. The bramble, especially, could easily survive in competition with the human race, and Anglo-Saxon town-dwellers may have been able to collect blackberries close to their homes. Raspberries, which are in any case found less frequently, are not quite so robust, but could easily be collected from the wild not far from towns. The Old English nomenclature of these fruits is confused, but the only possible reference to the fruits of either being consumed is a recipe in the *Lacnunga* for a laxative drink made of *bræmelberian*, 'bramble-berries'.[23] However, there is also confusion in Old English between brambles and briars, so even these could in fact be rose-hips. This is the only possible reference to the use of rose-hips, however. There are only two records of their seeds from archaeological sites, in contrast to the large numbers of the *Rubus* species, and the five 'hip'- place names only show that people noticed rose-hips, not that they ate them.

Gooseberries and blackcurrants were not cultivated, as far as we know, until the fifteenth century, so if they were eaten, it is most likely that they were gathered from the wild.[24] There is no evidence that they were cultivated or eaten in the Anglo-Saxon period, or even noticed: there is no known Old English name for either. However, this does not mean that people did not pick and eat them where they grew wild, and there is a rather enigmatic reference in the *Lacnunga* to a plant 'on which grow black berries just as big as other pea-beans'.[25] This sounds more like a blackcurrant than a blackberry in our sense, but the whole passage is obscure, and may even be a bad translation of something completely different.

EXOTIC FRUITS

There are references to peaches, medlars and mulberries (although the terminology is confused here too) in the medical texts, but no archaeological evidence to show that they (rather than just their names) were known in Anglo-Saxon England.[26] The one exotic fruit that certainly was known here is the grape. Pips have been found that may belong to imported dried fruit, but there is plenty of evidence that grapes were grown in Anglo-Saxon England, too.[27] Bede says in the introduction to his *Ecclesiastical History* that Britain had 'vineyards growing in certain places', although these places cannot have included eighth-century Northumbria where he was writing, and where the climate would not have been suitable.[28] However, there was a climatic amelioration towards the end of the period, and vines were planted in the south of England.[29] Planting vines is one of the *Gerefa*'s tasks for the spring (February to April), and by the time of Domesday Book, there were about forty-five vineyards in England, although some of them had been planted since 1066.[30]

DRINKS MADE FROM FRUIT

It is pretty clear that it was not for dessert grapes that vines were planted in early medieval England. The Old English vocabulary of wine, *win*, the vine, *wintreow* (literally 'wine-tree'), and the grape, *winberige* ('wine-berry'), shows which was most important to the Anglo-Saxons, and which they were familiar with first (very possibly before they left their Continental homelands). Wine would have been needed for the eucharist from the earliest days of the mission to the English, but it seems to have been in demand for recreational purposes from an early stage, too. No doubt the prestige of Mediterranean culture had a good deal to do with this. A letter from Alcuin (Charlemagne's schoolmaster) when he was visiting his native Northumbria in 790 shows the attitude of an English monk who had grown used to southern ways: 'Alas, alas, there is death in the pot, oh man of God, for there is no wine in our cups, and the bitter beer is savage in our bellies. And, because we have none, please drink in our name, and have a happy day ....'[31] Wine was thoroughly assimilated into secular ideas of 'a happy day', too, as this almost gnomic description from *Beowulf* shows: 'There was the best of feasts: men drank wine.'[32]

It is clear then that wine played an important part in Anglo-Saxon spiritual and intellectual life, but in everyday life it is likely that there was never as much wine as people would have liked (which would only have made it more desirable). The boy in Abbot Ælfric's *Colloquy* does not drink wine because 'I'm not so rich that I can buy wine for myself; and wine is not a drink for children or fools, but for the old and wise.'[33] Many other people must have been too poor too. Even monks, however old and wise, may not have drunk it as a matter of course: in the *Monasteriales indicia*, the sign for wine is listed among those needed in church, rather than the refectory, as in the contemporary continental lists, showing where English monks were more likely to encounter it.[34] However, there are signs in the *Indicia* for both 'dripped' wine, possibly a reduction to concentrate its sweetness, and a 'spice drink', which may have been based on wine too, both in the refectory section.[35] Anglo-Saxon monks may have been drinking some quite fancy drinks, but perhaps only on special occasions.

There is a certain amount of evidence that the Anglo-Saxons liked their wine sweet. The food rent that allows honey to be rendered as a substitute for wine certainly implies this, and so do the other alcoholic drinks they valued: generally, the sweeter it was the more they liked it. The Romans certainly valued the sweeter wines from the first pressing of the grapes more than the 'drier' ones produced later in the process, and also used wine boiled down to make it sweeter to fortify wine and make it keep longer.[36] There is no reason to suppose a break in wine production, although demand may have slackened with the end of the empire in the west, nor that tastes changed markedly. The wines imported into Anglo-Saxon England are therefore likely to have been essentially similar to those available in Roman Britain. Those made here were presumably modelled on the imported ones, although how successfully, we can only speculate.

Another drink included in the *Indicia* is *beor*, which looks as if it means 'beer', but the late Professor Fell showed that it indicates a drink made of or flavoured with fruit.[37] In one case it is equivalent to *æppelwin*, 'apple wine', so this may be the Old English word for cider. This may also be indicated by the *Indicia* sign, 'you grind your hand on the other', which might stand for milling or pressing apples.[38] Otherwise, the use of a French word in Modern English would suggest that cider was a post-Conquest introduction – Normandy is well known for its cider, after all. Whatever *beor* was, its name was used like those of wine, beer and mead to form compounds like 'beer-hall', 'mead-bench' and so on, showing that it was part of the normal repertoire of Anglo-Saxon alcoholic drinks, and considered suitable for feasting.

USES OF FRUIT

Before sugar was in widespread use, fruit could not be bottled or made into jam. Some might be dried, but most fruits would have to be eaten fresh, and would therefore only be available for a short time: strawberries in June, blackberries in August and September, and so on. These may simply have been picked as they were found, much as we still do blackberries. Where we have evidence of cultivation, however, as in the case of apples, pears and plums, varieties may have been developed to extend the cropping season. Charlemagne's apple varieties included earlies, and among his pears were late ones, and it is possible that these tendencies were also exploited on this side of the Channel. Also in both lists were *servatoria*, 'keepers'; if this possibility was taken advantage of in England, apples and pears could have been available for a considerable part of the winter. Apples (there is much less evidence for pears, so they are unlikely to have been so important) might therefore form quite a significant element in the diet, contributing vitamin C and the only substantial amount of sugars, apart from those in fermented drinks. No doubt they were appreciated for their sweet taste (by Ælfric Bata's schoolboys, for instance), even though their nutritional role was not understood.

It is unlikely that fruit was cooked much: the great British pudding, and the whole tradition of finishing meals with a sweet dish, also depends on the availability of sugar. There was little tradition of cooking with honey before sugar came in; conserves were occasionally made with honey as an alternative to sugar in the later Middle Ages,[39] but there is no reason to project this back four or five hundred years into the Anglo-Saxon period. As discussed in the last chapter, most honey is likely to have gone into mead production. Fruits could have been used to flavour *briw*, or indeed bread, but there is no evidence for it. Those that were too sour to eat raw, or the good parts of those that were going off, might have been combined with other ingredients, rather than let them go to waste, but again this is supposition. Fresh fruit would mainly be available in the summer, when cooked food would not be needed to warm people up, so most of it was probably eaten raw. Given the Anglo-Saxon attitude to honey and grapes, though, it may be that a lot of fruit was consumed as *beor*, rather than in its original state.

NUTS

Even better keeping than apples and pears are nuts. The only native nuts usually eaten by humans are hazelnuts (*Corylus avellana*), and these, or their shells, are quite frequent in archaeological remains.[40] They could have made quite an important contribution to people's diet, and would have kept right through the winter. They are the most common shrub in lowland deciduous woodland, providing useful crops of coppice poles, and so there will have been plenty of nuts to collect.[41] The same woods would provide beechnuts and acorns from standard trees. These are likely to have been eaten in times of dearth, but even in good years they would have made a contribution to human nutrition as the mast on which pigs were fed in the autumn.[42] Of the more exotic nuts, there is a little evidence that walnuts (*Juglans regia*) were eaten, and finds of the wood presumably represent trees grown here, but the name *wealh-hnutu*, 'foreign nut', suggests that they were not grown in England commonly enough to be accepted as English.[43] A single walnut was found in a female burial at West Heslerton in Yorkshire, mounted in metal strips as if it was regarded as an amulet.[44] This suggests that walnuts were rare enough to be credited with magical or quasi-magical powers. Chestnut wood has also been found, suggesting that the trees were growing here, but no nuts, and there is no written evidence that they were eaten, or even known.[45] As they are rather unpleasant raw, it may be that the knowledge of how to prepare them had not been imported along with the trees. Almonds and pine-nuts are mentioned very occasionally in the medical texts, but there are no archaeological finds, and both are described in such a way as to suggest they were not familiar to writer or readers.[46] It is possible that they were just names, and never really used. The elaborate use of almond products in 'fish-day' recipes certainly belongs to a later period.[47] However, they could have been imported in small quantities as part of the spice trade without making any impression on the archaeological record. Overall, however, the average Anglo-Saxon is much more likely to have eaten hazelnuts than any others. Only the rich would have access to imported nuts, and only the very poor would eat acorns or beechnuts, and then only in a dire emergency. The season for hazelnuts begins in late August, and they are ripe by the end of September.[48] Since they keep so well, nuts may have been a Christmas treat in Anglo-Saxon England as they are today.

~ FOUR &~

PROTEIN FROM THE LAND
Meat, Dairy Products and Eggs

In the modern affluent west, few people are at risk of protein deficiency (excess fat from 'protein' foods is much more of a problem). But the same is not true in poor countries, and it was not true in Anglo-Saxon England, either. For this reason, animal foods were particularly valued, and herds of cattle were the main form of movable wealth. Children are particularly vulnerable to poor nutrition, and skeletal studies have shown that a high proportion (a quarter to a half) of Anglo-Saxons had suffered some kind of nutritional crisis in childhood.[1] Greater precision is not possible, since malnutrition mainly affects the soft tissues, but scurvy and rickets, which do leave distinctive signs on the skeleton, are not common.[2] The 'mortalities of cattle' sporadically reported in the *Anglo-Saxon Chronicle*[3] must have resulted in shortages of meat, however, and, although it is likely that large animals such as bullocks were mainly eaten by the upper classes, it is not likely that they would be affected by shortages more than the poor. In other words, if only less desirable forms of animal food were available, they were almost certainly eaten by those at the top of the social scale, leaving those lower down with less than they needed.

DAIRY GOODS

In Anglo-Saxon England, milk came not only from cows, but from sheep and goats as well. In Ælfric's *Colloquy*, it is the shepherd who complains about having to milk and make cheese and butter, as well as look after his flock: '... at the crack of dawn I drive my sheep to pasture, and I stand over them in heat and cold with my dogs, so that wolves don't devour them,

53

21 *Men milking ewes in Greece in the twentieth century.* After Jessica Kuper, *The Anthropologist's Cookbook*, Kegan Paul 1997

and I take them back to their folds, and milk them twice a day, and move their folds, and on top of that I make cheese and butter; and I'm faithful to my lord.'[4] In the *Rectitudines singularum personarum*, there are people responsible for cows, goats and sheep, but cheese and butter are made by a specialist (interestingly, the only explicitly female worker in the text). Goatherd and shepherd are entitled to whey or buttermilk from their flocks, however, showing that these consisted of dairy animals.[5] The most numerous dairy animals were undoubtedly sheep, as very large flocks existed by the end of our period, but, even so, more milk probably came from cows, which have a higher yield than sheep, or even goats.[6] In early medieval Ireland, a cow's annual yield was worth 18d, a goat's 1⅓d, and a ewe's only ½d or ⅓d.[7] Nearly all our evidence comes from large estates with specialist workers; we know little about what dairy animals peasant farmers kept, or even relatively humble landlords, but the cowherd in the *Rectitudines* was allowed to keep his own 'food-cow' (presumably for milking) with his lord's.[8]

Fresh milk was probably a relatively unimportant product of the dairy flocks and herds. Partly due to a shortage of fresh fodder, all milking animals would normally go dry during the winter, so fresh milk was only a seasonal food. Even the rich, who could afford better feed for their animals, would not be able to keep them in milk, as year-round milking is not a natural characteristic of any of these animals, but has been consistently promoted by breeders.[9] Even now, sheep do not normally give milk right through the winter.[10] Milk was certainly drunk, and no doubt it was appreciated when it was in plentiful supply; Bede says that the Old English name for the month of May was *thrimilchi*, 'three-milk', although he regards this abundance as belonging to a time before his own.[11] Much of this early summer glut must have been turned into cheese and butter, however, to preserve it for the dark days of winter, and thus fresh milk was not a standard part of people's diet as it is today. There is a sign in the *Indicia*, suggesting that it was drunk in monasteries when available.[12] It also features in the second Bury funeral feast, so it may have been seen as something of a luxury, suitable for the privileged, or special occasions. Alternatively, perhaps it was considered especially appropriate for monks, because they were not supposed to eat meat.

The milk of different animals may have been used for different purposes. For instance, cream rises easily to the surface of cows' milk, but much more slowly from that of sheep and goats. This makes cows' milk more suitable for making butter, and leads to the temptation to make cheese from the skimmed milk, and thus get two products for one. Ewes' and goats' milk, on the other hand, is more easily made into cheese and, with its butterfat intact, gives a richer result. All this was well understood in seventeenth-century Scotland, where 'cheiss of kys milk' was considered a very inferior product, but unfortunately we have no evidence that such distinctions were observed in early medieval England.[13] It is possible that goat's milk was considered easier to digest, and therefore appropriate to invalid diet.

Of the products made from milk, cheese seems to have been the priority, rather than butter. In the *Rectitudines*, the cheese-maker makes cheese first, and then butter for her lord's table out of the whey. She keeps what remains, once the shepherd and goatherd have had their share. The cheese is therefore made from full-cream milk, concentrating the milk-solids into one product. This may be because hard cheese, at least, keeps better than butter, and is thus a safer repository for all that goodness. On the other hand, since the dairy-worker was making cheese for her employer out of his own milk, keeping qualities may not have been all that important. It might be easier to interpret these arrangements if we knew which animals' milk she was using, or even if any distinction was being made. At least some Anglo-Saxon cheese, that made by tenants for their landlords, must have been hard, as it features quite regularly in their food rents, which consist almost entirely of foods that are easy to store.[14] What kind of cheese they made for their own consumption, if indeed they had enough milk to do so, we do not know. The sign in the *Indicia* is for a small cheese; small cheeses would not keep as long as larger ones, but the sign may refer to cheese made within monasteries for fairly immediate consumption.[15] Store cheeses for all landlords may have come from their tenants.

Unfortunately, we know virtually nothing about the eating qualities of Anglo-Saxon cheese. *Bald's Leechbook* refers to 'old cheese' as part of an invalid diet, which has rather fancifully been interpreted as mouldy cheese, for its supposed antibiotic properties, but is more likely to be mature cheese that had been stored. No doubt some cheeses would develop moulds and become 'blue' in store, but there is no clear reference to this. We do not know whether this development would have been welcomed, let alone deliberately promoted. In fact, there is no evidence that the Anglo-Saxons recognised, still less valued, different types of cheese, or those from different parts of the country. The reputations of certain regions for rich pastures and high-quality dairying must be a later development.

Turning to butter, making it from whey, rather than cream, might seem rather parsimonious to us, but it may be that any butter was a luxury in early medieval England. It is said specifically to be for the lord's table, so it is evidently not considered a low-grade product. No butter is being made for sale, nor apparently for consumption by servants, unless these were lucky enough to eat with their lord. In the *Indicia*, the sign is for 'butter or fat' (probably lard), showing that even the privileged did not eat butter all the time.[16] Perhaps they kept it for special occasions, or ate it only in season. By the end of the period, there was some limited commercial production, as 'women who deal in cheese and butter' are mentioned among traders in London.[17] These are the kind of moderately long-keeping items whose production might expand with the growth of markets and trade. The women paid their toll before Christmas, which may have been when there was most demand.

It appears that the cheese-maker, shepherd and goatherd were drinking whey or buttermilk instead of fresh milk. It may be that this was what Anglo-Saxon peasants generally drank, when they weren't drinking beer. In Iceland in more recent centuries, the ordinary people only drank beer on special occasions; their everyday drink was *blanda*, made by diluting sour whey.[18] This drink was also traditional in the Northern Isles,[19] but we have no evidence for it in early medieval England. The boy in Ælfric's *Colloquy* says he drinks water if he has no beer.[20] Sour whey was also used as a preservative in Iceland, in preference to salt.[21] However, there is no evidence for this economical technique in Anglo-Saxon England either.

Various types of soured and curdled milk, whole or skimmed, were used in Iceland and the Isles as well, and similar traditions have existed elsewhere in Scandinavia and in Scotland.[22] These shared traditions are usually attributed to the Vikings, and if this explanation is correct, it ought to apply to parts of England as well. Alternatively, these may simply be sensible ways of using the products of flocks and herds where these are the main source of nourishment, that is to say in northern Europe. In this case, too, one would expect them to have recommended themselves in upland parts of England. The lack of Anglo-Saxon evidence for all these 'secondary' milk products may reflect their status as food for the poor, or the early disappearance of such traditions in England, or it may be that they really never were in use here.

FOWL AND EGGS

The domestic poultry of Anglo-Saxon England were chickens and geese; ducks were not domesticated until later in the Middle Ages.[23] That does not mean ducks were not eaten, however; mallards were probably as common as they are now, and other species of wild duck would have been available in some localities. Ælfric's fowler says he catches birds with nets, traps, lime, hawks and by whistling, which would give him access to a wide range of species, but unfortunately he does not say which they were.[24] 'Ordinary Anglo-Saxons' might not use such a variety of techniques as this specialist, but they would undoubtedly have caught birds, including ducks, for their own use. The role of poultry in Anglo-Saxon diet is not clear; they do not feature in those few feasts of which we have records, so it may be that they were not special-occasion food. On the other hand, gutting and plucking a bird, especially a goose, is a substantial task, unlikely to have been undertaken on a daily basis, at least in peasant households. Peasants may also have valued their poultry more highly, not having so many larger animals to choose from. The Mexican proverb, 'A poor man only eats chicken if he's sick or the chicken was,' may have applied equally to Anglo-Saxon England. Chicken soup is mentioned as invalid food in *Bald's Leechbook*.[25]

Eggs, like milk, were a seasonal food. The hen that lays all the year round was not even a dream at this period. The spring glut no doubt accounts for the association of eggs with Easter at the present day, and this may go back to the Anglo-Saxon period. In suitable areas, the eggs of wild birds must have been collected, too. Ducks are especially suited to this mode of exploitation, as they lay large eggs, and do not look after them particularly well. The eggs of wild birds have their seasons, too, shorter because they are more easily discouraged from laying if they are not able to hatch their eggs. Nevertheless, large numbers may well have been collected in favourable areas, if not quite as enormous as recorded from the Scottish islands and cliffs in more recent times.[26] What then was done with all these eggs? They cannot all have been eaten at once. Preservation methods like the bran-tub may have been in use, but, without refrigeration, eggs cannot have been kept for long periods of time.

We do have a little information about the cooking of eggs. 'Beaten eggs', possibly scrambled, are invalid food in *Bald's Leechbook*.[27] Whether they were also eaten by healthy people is not clear. In the *Indicia*, the sign for an egg mimics picking off the shell, implying that it was in hard-boiled form that they normally appeared in monastic refectories.[28]

MEAT

The Bury funeral lists ask for a bullock (beef), bucks (venison) and a pig (pork), as well as a flitch of bacon. This gives the impression that game played quite an important part in the Anglo-Saxon diet. The upper classes certainly enjoyed hunting, and also employed huntsmen to supply them with game when they could not themselves hunt (or were unsuccessful).[29] There is a huntsman in Ælfric's *Colloquy*, who lists the animals he catches as red, fallow[30] and roe deer, boar and sometimes hares.[31] The remains of these species, apart from fallow deer, are found in archaeology, most commonly red deer, but, overall, game rarely amounts to more than five per cent of bones on any one site.[32] Even for the aristocracy, then, domestic animals are likely to have been much more significant in the diet than wild ones. Game may have been considered particularly appropriate for feasting, and hunting may have been a winter activity as it is at the present day. At particular meals (at Christmas, for example), therefore, game might have been a significant element, perhaps the main type of meat, for the upper classes, while remaining a minor factor if the year is taken as whole.

Of the domestic animals, more sheep bones are found than any other species.[33] This may not mean that more mutton was eaten than beef, for instance, because a sheep carcass is much smaller than an ox. The proportion of goats is hard to estimate, because most of their bones are indistinguishable from those of sheep. However, extrapolating from those bones that can be told apart (chiefly the skull), it is clear that sheep were much more common than goats. Figures for East Anglia in Domesday Book show that the distribution of goats was quite uneven. Some estates may have specialised in them, either for commercial purposes, or because their vegetation was more suitable for these browsing animals than the grazing sheep. Some people may therefore have eaten goat quite often, others perhaps not at all. Sheep appear to have been much more ubiquitous, but it is striking (in as far as such a limited sample means anything) that they do not feature in the Bury funeral feasts. It may be that mutton was not considered suitable for special meals, at least by those prosperous enough to have a choice.

Pigs are not as numerous as cattle or sheep, but huge herds were kept on some estates.[34] Some woods in Domesday Book are measured by the number of swine they could support,[35] so it seems likely that pigs were kept in large numbers for commercial reasons; the numbers are too large to be for household use, even for very rich households. Some high-status sites do yield substantial amounts of pig bone, though, showing that pig meat was far from despised by the wealthy. The pig certainly does not seem to have been the cottager's animal that it was in more recent centuries. It must have been valued for the same reasons, however, namely its ability to subsist on free food (beech-mast and acorns in the Middle Ages, kitchen waste more recently), and its suitability for curing (salting, smoking, or both), which meant that it could be stored for long periods after slaughter. This last virtue was certainly exploited: a side of bacon is mentioned in the Bury will fragment, and they also feature in food rents.[36]

Such an economical animal was no doubt kept by the less prosperous, too, and exploited to the full, although perhaps not quite to the extent it was later, when 'everything except the squeak' was said to be eaten. Despite extensive research, I have been able to find no evidence for the Anglo-Saxon sausage; in fact in one glossary entry, *lucanica*, a type of sausage, is explained as *mearh*, marrow.[37] However, this may only mean that this particular type of sausage was unfamiliar, not the whole concept. It seems *a priori* unlikely that such economical expedients as black pudding and haggis were unknown. Nonetheless, it has to be said that there is no evidence for them this early, unless a reference

22 *Killing a pig at Papa Westray, Orkney, 1930s.* After Fenton, *Northern Isles*

to 'a hundred sides of bacon and all the *smean* that go with them' is relevant.[38] *Smean* is usually translated 'delicacies', and taken to mean things to eat with the bacon, but it is hard to know what these might be. If it was taken to mean 'products' instead, it might stand for all the other things made from a pig when it was killed primarily to make bacon.[39]

It might be thought that the *Monasteriales indicia* and Ælfric's *Colloquy* would be no use to us in investigating Anglo-Saxon meat consumption, since monks were supposed to eschew the flesh of quadrupeds. But Ælfric's pupils were not yet under this prohibition: the discussion of diet is prefaced by a boy's explanation that 'I still eat meat, because I'm a boy living under the rod.'[40] When he is a monk living under the Rule, he will have to give it up. Even then, though, there may be some limited occasions when he will be allowed meat: the *Indicia* has a sign 'If you need salt meat for any reason.'[41] Evidently, in a reformed monastery, you needed a reason, but unfortunately we are not told what this might be. One would be sickness, which is allowed for in St Benedict's Rule. The fact that salt meat only is referred to might suggest that the custom had not yet begun of monks having their blood let every year and being allowed meat while they recovered.[42] Salt meat would be most suitable where it needed to be stored for long periods and was only required in small quantities; if it was being used on a regular basis or in large quantities, it might be worth acquiring fresh, or having animals slaughtered. Presumably all monastic estates would be producing animals suitable for slaughter (and the communities would need their other products, milk, wool, hides, traction, lard, etc.); how these were disposed of we do not know, but they would give estate managers and cellarers a considerable resource with which to buy other luxuries.

One big question is whether there was a major autumn slaughter of domestic animals in Anglo-Saxon England. Bede's Old English name for November, 'blood-month', might imply this,[43] and winter feed would certainly be at a premium. However, archaeological remains show that most animals had several years of life before they were slaughtered, suggesting that substantial flocks and herds were kept on through the winter. The bones also suggest that Anglo-Saxon farm animals were generally well fed and healthy, so there seems to have been enough fodder for those animals that were kept.[44] The answer may be that stocking levels were very low by later standards. However, in many ways it would make sense to slaughter animals in cold weather rather than hot: fresh meat would keep for longer, allowing large carcasses such as oxen to be eaten before they became dangerous. The best time to kill pigs would be at the end of the autumn, after they had fattened up on wood-pasture, and pig-killing is certainly a winter task from the later Middle Ages onwards. It may be then that more fresh meat was eaten during the winter than in the summer, although bacon and other preserved pig products would keep right through the year. More would certainly be eaten by rich people than poor, and the 'best' animals would be kept for special occasions. For the poor, this might mean any animals at all (poultry, wildfowl, pigs?), while the aristocracy certainly favoured game. Beef, as we have seen above, may have been preferred over mutton, and young animals may also have been seen as a treat.

What was Anglo-Saxon meat like? The age-at-slaughter figures suggest that most of it would have been quite mature, and therefore probably tough. An ox at the end of his working life would certainly be a daunting prospect, and a retired milking cow, or a sheep that had yielded several clips of wool would not be tender, either. Even pigs, usually killed in their second or third year, would be more mature than we are used to. If most meat was relatively tough, young animals, lamb and veal especially, may have been particularly welcome when they were available. The symbolic association between lambs and Easter may have been reflected at the table. All Anglo-Saxon domestic animals were smaller than modern ones, size being one of the factors favoured by breeders of all species.[45] This need not affect the eating quality of the meat, but would certainly mean that more work was expended to yield a given amount of meat. At the present day, it is usually maintained that more 'primitive' breeds of livestock, reared more slowly than modern ones, give more tender and better-flavoured meat;[46] if this was true of Anglo-Saxon animals, it may have mitigated the ill effects of later age at slaughter.

As well as meat, an important product of slaughtered animals was fat, especially lard from pigs. This was the main cooking fat; oil can only have been imported in tiny quantities, and butter, as we have seen, was a luxury. Monks were allowed to use lard, especially in the winter, even though meat was forbidden.[47] Anthimus, writing in sixth-century Gaul, identified *laridum* as a 'Frankish delicacy'. This is almost certainly bacon, not lard, but he says that its fat is poured over vegetables when no oil is available.[48] The implication is that pig-fat of some kind is a northern European (or Germanic?) equivalent to Mediterranean olive oil. The terminology of fats in Old English is complex and unclear, so it is often hard to tell whether lard or the fat of some other animal is meant. The main reason for believing that lard was the most important is the large amount of fat on a pig carcass. Anglo-Saxon pigs may not have been as fat as modern breeds, but they must still have been fat in comparison to other animals.[49] The poet Aldhelm's great riddle on 'Creation' shows that pigs were proverbially fat around the year 700: 'I grow fatter by far than the fat of sows / when once more they bring their bodies to the mast-bearing beeches / and delight the swineherd with their fattened flesh.'[50] There is also the traditional role of lard in more recent English diet. In the nineteenth century, William Cobbett complained that the rural poor were beginning to think themselves above eating bread and lard, but it was used until well into the twentieth century where oil, butter or margarine might be used now.[51] The fat of other species is occasionally mentioned, for instance in medical recipes, but undifferentiated references to *smeoru*, etc. must usually have meant lard in practice. As well as food, it would be used for greasing harness and similar household jobs, but that leads us outside our topic. All the same, it does help to emphasise the absolutely central role of livestock in Anglo-Saxon life.

～ FIVE ～

FOOD FROM THE WATERS
Fish and Seafood

Despite the growing importance of trade and money towards the end of the period, the Anglo-Saxon economy was still based on subsistence. In such an economy, most fish is eaten near where it is caught, and thus the role of fish in the diet is much more important along the coast and major estuaries than inland. Freshwater fish from rivers mean that there will be pockets of higher fish consumption in the interior, but these will be so local that they are unlikely to make much impression on the overall pattern. By the end of our period, there does seem to have been a trade in preserved fish,[1] presumably allowing those away from fishing areas to eat fish on fast days, but this will not have affected the vast majority of the population: only town-dwellers, ecclesiastical establishments and the aristocracy are likely to have been using money to buy food on any scale. Even at the end of the Anglo-Saxon period, the vast majority of the population lived outside towns, made their living from the land, and probably entered into the money economy only in so far as they were required to in order to pay rent and taxes. In other words, the fishmonger's customers were the privileged. If 'ordinary Anglo-Saxons' ate fish, that was probably because it was free; they could catch it themselves in nearby rivers, lakes or the sea. On some parts of the coast, where conditions for farming might not be very good, some people may have eaten more fish than anything else, as in parts of Scotland quite recently.[2] In inland areas, where there was no reliable supply of freshwater fish, a tradition of fishing may never have developed, and thus people may have eaten none at all.

Fish also have their seasons. Shellfish are traditionally eaten 'when there is an R in the month', that is to say, not in the summer, and, perhaps not by coincidence, the two great fasts enjoined by the Church, Advent and Lent, fall in the winter and spring respectively (in fact, the word 'Lent' originally meant 'spring'). The herring fisheries of recent centuries followed the

63

migrations of the shoals from the north of Scotland down to East Anglia;[3] in our period, with smaller boats, they must have waited till the fish came to them. Fasts, not only seasonal but weekly, must have meant a much greater demand for fish than would otherwise have existed. Fish would have been used as a substitute for meat whenever this was forbidden (and by those who could have afforded it if it was allowed). Religious communities must always have been the biggest customers. At least in the wake of the reforms of the tenth century, monks were not supposed to eat meat at all, and so there would be a demand for fish from them all the year round.

SHELLFISH

Eating seafood would be encouraged among the clergy, too, but this passage from the (probably late) Anglo-Saxon poem *Seasons for Fasting* shows that this depended on the circumstances:

> But I can say,   tearful with sorrows,
> how the priests   make trouble again
> every day,   anger the Lord
> and maliciously   lead astray every
> one of the people   who is willing to follow them;
> first thing in the morning they   sing mass,
> and, consumed,   led on, by thirst,
> after the tapster   they haul through the streets.
> Look! They deceitfully   start lying
> and keep egging on   the tapster,
> say that without sin   he can give them
> oysters to eat   and noble wine
> during the morning,   so that it seems to me
> that dog and wolf   act the same
> way in the world,   and do not know
> when they will get food,   having no moderation.
> Then, sitting down, they   begin to weary,
> bless the wine,   keep giving it out,
> say 'Good life'   to each of the men,
> that any man   is allowed
> after he takes mass,   tired, to take wine,
> also eat oysters   and other
> fish from the water ...[4]

1 Top: Leactun: *kale growing under netting in the recreated Anglo-Saxon vegetable garden at Bede's World, Jarrow, Tyne and Wear, May 2003. All the vegetables grown here are chosen to be as close as possible to the varieties that were available in Bede's lifetime in the eighth century. Although there is no evidence for the use of nets in the Anglo-Saxon period, some measures must have been taken to stop birds eating the leafy vegetables.* Author

2 Above left: *Vine-scroll: cross-shaft at Bakewell parish church, Derbyshire, probably tenth century. The number of Anglo-Saxon sculptural fragments found here shows that this was a major church in the early Middle Ages.* Author

3 Above right: *Inhabited vine-scroll: part of the early eighth-century cross at Bewcastle in Cumbria. Such motifs derive ultimately from Byzantine art, and, although they reveal a good deal about Anglo-Saxon artistic affinities and aspirations, they cannot tell us what plants or animals were familiar to the artist.* Author

4 Above left: *Reconstructed single-chamber oven at West Stow Anglo-Saxon Village, Suffolk, spring 2003. The wooden peels leaning against the side are used to put loaves into the hot oven and take them out when cooked. In England these ovens have to be built under some kind of shelter, otherwise they rapidly collapse.* Author

5 Above right: *Carbonised loaves from an eleventh-century house at Buttermarket, Ipswich. These finds are unique.* Copyright Suffolk County Council Archaeological Service

6 Below: *Hops from Kent, September 2003. The 'cones' (foreground) are the part used to flavour beer.* Author

7 *Field beans,* Vicia faba *var.* minor, *grown in Cambridge, 1995.* Author

8 *Wild cabbage growing at the Cambridge Botanic Garden, 1994.* Author

9 Above: *White carrot grown in Cambridge, 1998.* Author

10 Left: *Wild beets at Cambridge Botanic Garden, 1994.* Author

Opposite page:
11 Above left: *Apple var. Decio growing at the National Fruit Collection, Brogdale, Kent, 1992. Although this variety may not in fact go back to the Roman period, it is very small for a cultivated variety, and must resemble the apples that grew in Anglo-Saxon England.* Author

12 Above right: *Wild pear growing at Brogdale. The fruit is minute and very hard, probably not worth picking and eating, even when it was the only kind of pear available.* Author

13 Below left: *Wardon pear at Brogdale. This is a medieval variety, although almost certainly post-Conquest.* Author

14 Below right: *Bullace (*Prunus insititia*) growing in the hedgerow at Wicken Fen, Cambridgeshire, 1983. These may have an admixture of genetic material from modern cultivars, but nevertheless both trees and fruit would be familiar to an Anglo-Saxon.* Author

15 Above left: *Medlars* (Mespilus germanica) *growing at Cambridge, 1991. The only reason to think that medlars were more than a name to the Anglo-Saxons is that the name concerned,* openærs, *describes the fruit's shape quite accurately.* Author

16 Above right: *Grapevine, var. Wrotham Pinot, growing in the recreated medieval garden at Winchester Castle, 1993. This variety probably goes back to the Middle Ages, although not as far as the Anglo-Saxon period.* Author

17 *Yearling Soay lambs at Wimpole Home Farm, spring 2003. This is the only British breed of sheep completely unaffected by eighteenth-century improvement, having been isolated on the St Kilda group of islands in the Atlantic until the 1930s. In fact it is probably more primitive than Anglo-Saxon sheep, as it is impossible to herd with dogs, and jumps like a goat.* Author

18 *Herdwick ram at Bede's World, Jarrow, May 2003. Although Herdwicks have been influenced to some extent by 'scientific' breeding, they remain a much hardier breed, able to thrive on less rich pasture, than modern lowland sheep.* Author

19 *Dexter ox at Bede's World, Jarrow, May 2003. Dexter cattle have been deliberately dwarfed to produce a 'cottager's cow'. This has not necessarily resulted in an ideal ox for ploughing, but he is about the same size as his Anglo-Saxon equivalent.* Author

20 *Tamworth pigs at Ryton Organic Gardens, Warwickshire, 1995. The Tamworth is the least 'improved' of British pig breeds; note the long snout.* Author

21 *Wild swine–Tamworth cross sow at West Stow Anglo-Saxon Village, Suffolk, spring 2003. Cross-breeding Tamworths with wild swine produces a pig similar in size and proportion to Anglo-Saxon ones, although probably the wrong colour.* Author

What the priests are being berated for here is casual eating (as well as drinking). The reference to dogs and wolves shows that what the poet objects to is the indiscriminate nature of their consumption, unrelated to the ecclesiastical timetable or the ceremony of formal feasting. What is perhaps more interesting from the point of view of the history of food and eating, however, is that they are apparently (once they have convinced him it is not sinful) able to buy oysters (and possibly other fish) from the same retailer as wine. There are a few other Anglo-Saxon references to drinking houses, but this is the only clue that food could also be bought there. That oysters are the specified Anglo-Saxon equivalent of *tapas* is also interesting, since these seem to have been very commonly eaten in early medieval England (far from being the luxury they are now, oysters were still cheap food in the early twentieth century).[5] One of the *Exeter Book* riddles deals with the apprehension of an oyster as its hour of consumption draws near.[6] Many of the riddles seem rather obscure to the modern reader, but it does appear that they were at least intended to be accessible to contemporaries, suggesting that the oyster was a familiar article of diet. This supposition is supported by the *Monasteriales indicia*: unlike later monastic sign lists, it does not have a long list of signs for different kinds of fish; following the general sign for fish, there are just two, for eels and oysters.[7] We know that monastic houses received enormous numbers of eels in their food rents (see below), so this pairing may suggest that monks ate oysters in large quantities too.

It is a pity that we do not have a more detailed account of the fish eaten in Anglo-Saxon monasteries, since they formed such an important part of the monks' diet, or at least were supposed to. That we do not may mean that other species of fish were not eaten in such large numbers as oysters and eels, or that different types were not distinguished in the same way as these two rather anomalous ones. Among shellfish, there is certainly no evidence that any other kind was as popular as oysters, but presumably others were eaten, at least on the coast and along estuaries where they were available for the picking. Ælfric's *Colloquy* mentions mussels, winkles and cockles, as well as oysters.[8] It must always be remembered that this text is largely a vocabulary exercise, but it is unlikely that Abbot Ælfric would have included these shellfish solely so that his pupils could translate their Latin names, if they were never likely to see the real thing. Winkles with peas and shellfish in soup are recommended in *Bald's Leechbook* as being easy to digest.[9]

FRESHWATER FISH

The same would apply to the other fish listed in the *Colloquy*. Among freshwater fish, as far as I have been able to translate them, these are: 'Eels and pike(?) and minnows and burbot/eel-pout(?) and trout and lampreys, and whatever kind is swimming in the river.'[10] This last comment suggests that the precise distinctions between different species of fish were not all that important to the Anglo-Saxons.[11] At West Stow, the early settlement site near Bury St Edmunds, the overwhelming majority of fish bones came from pike and perch, almost certainly from the nearby River Lark.[12] However, this may be a sentiment that Ælfric attributes to the fisherman, rather than one he or his pupils would agree with. He may have thought that fishermen did not have much discrimination, or were too lazy to seek out desirable species. At any rate, there is little sign that particular fish were being selected, let alone 'cultivated'. Nor is there evidence that the elaborate systems of fishponds associated with monasteries after the Conquest existed in the Anglo-Saxon period.[13] Their development probably went along with the increasingly sophisticated taste for a varied repertoire of fish as upper-class 'fasting' fare in the post-Conquest period. Ælfric's fisherman is fairly perfunctory on techniques for catching fish: 'I get in my boat and put my nets on the water, and throw out my hook for my baskets'. As well as these methods, both documentary references and archaeological remains suggest that fish-weirs made of wattle panels played an

23 This wattle structure, found in the mud of the Deben estuary below Sutton Hoo, is almost certainly a fish-weir. After Linzi Everett in Saxon *38, 2003*

important part.[14] These would not select particular species, of course, but since they did not kill the fish, it would be possible to let any undesirable ones go. The most desirable had to be kept for the landowner.[15]

SEA FISH

Whatever Abbot Ælfric thought of the judgement of fishermen, he certainly did not credit them with much spirit of adventure, for when he asks 'Why don't you fish in the sea?' the boy playing the fisherman is made to reply: 'Sometimes I do, but not often, because it's a long voyage for me to the sea.' However, he is persuaded to list some marine species – 'herrings and salmon, dolphins and sturgeon, oysters and crabs, ... plaice and flounder and lobster and lots like that'[16] – and again these may have been mainly fish that Ælfric's pupils would be familiar with in real life. Dolphin and sturgeon, however, are more likely to have graced royal tables than monastic ones. In King Æthelræd's regulations for the port of London, *craspisce*, literally 'fat fish', is associated with wine as a luxury import that attracts a huge toll of 6s, as well as a twentieth part of the fish (cf. the toll on an ordinary shipload of fish below).[17] This fat fish was undoubtedly a cetacean of some kind, but when Ælfric's fisherman is asked whether he would like to catch a whale, he replies that he would rather catch a fish he can kill than one which could drown or kill not only him but his companions too with one stroke.[18] There seems to be a demarcation here between the cautious fisherman and the more enterprising types who venture on the high seas.

The question remains, however, how much sea fish really reached monasteries, let alone anyone else, in inland districts. The *Colloquy* may owe its origin to Ælfric's monastic training at Winchester, not a coastal town, but one that is believed to still have had close trading links with nearby Southampton. By the time the text was written down he was probably at Cerne Abbas,[19] not much further away from the sea. All monasteries, wherever they were, must have needed mechanisms, probably involving both trade and rents, to ensure supplies of fish, and many of them held coastal estates. Ælfric's fisherman goes onto say that he sells his fish in the town and can sell all he can catch.[20] He is not therefore intended to represent someone supplying a monastery directly, but monastic cellarers or factors might be among his customers. Winchester and Cerne would be within a few hours' journey by cart of the coast, and might therefore receive fresh fish from the sea, but other religious foundations, further inland, would rely on fish that had been preserved in some way.

PRESERVED FISH

One fish that is not mentioned in the *Colloquy*, but nevertheless seems to have been important, is cod. Both cod and herring figure largely in the 'stored fish industry' that can be traced back to the tenth century. At this early stage, herring is dominant, but cod and its relatives are a close second.[21] If cod was only eaten in 'stored', or preserved, form, this might explain why it is not listed by the fisherman; only fish that were eaten fresh would be associated with him. No fish are mentioned by Ælfric's merchant, who seems to deal in luxury goods only, but Æthelræd's London regulations include a toll of a penny on a shipload of fish (or a halfpenny on a boatload), presumably from overseas, as well as the *craspisce* mentioned above.[22] These fish must have been preserved in some way, unless they were expected to be consumed more or less immediately by the citizens. There is evidence for preserved fish penetrating quite a long way inland in the 'Ely Farming Memoranda', which list the provisions made by that abbey for the foundation of another one at Thorney in the 970s. The very first item of expenditure mentioned is 2,000 herrings for 40d.[23] Unfortunately we are not told where the herrings are to be purchased.

How these stored fish were preserved is not totally clear; the only method for which there is good evidence is salting – there is a salter in Ælfric's *Colloquy*, although he does not mention fish among the foods that would be lost without him.[24] Unfortunately we do not have enough evidence to tell whether foods were preserved with dry salt or brine, or both, or which was the more common method. Salting (by whichever method) may well have been the main commercial means of preservation, but methods like drying and smoking, which are effectively free, may have been more popular with households preserving fish on a small scale for their own use or for sale locally. (Although salt would be available on the coast free of money payment, there was still considerable labour involved in processing it.) Both drying and smoking are traditional in Scotland and Scandinavia, where many economical and self-sufficient food–ways remained in use long after they had been abandoned in England.[25]

We can be sure that familiar types of preserved fish such as kippers and bloaters (both starting life as herring) were not available to the Anglo-Saxons, as these are both relatively recent inventions.[26] Types of preserved herring that were produced in England in the Middle Ages were dried (which may have been lightly smoked too), white (i.e. salted, either in dry salt or brine, after gutting), and red (salted without gutting, and then smoked for up to four weeks).[27] Other types of smoked fish might have

24 *Drying fish on the beach near Lerwick, Shetland, late nineteenth century?* After Fenton,
Northern Isles

been salmon and eel.[28] Eel were rendered in thousands and even tens of
thousands in Domesday Book.[29] There is no reason to suppose that the
new Norman upper classes were particularly devoted to this species, and
indeed similar renders were paid in the Anglo-Saxon period (if not so sys-
tematically recorded).[30] The vast numbers involved suggest that some kind
of preservation must have been used. These cannot have been the live eels
that until recently frightened children on fishmongers' counters, unless
some extensive system of waterworks was in existence to store them, and,
as we have seen, this technology seems to have been in its infancy.

OTHER MARINE PRODUCTS

Apart from fish, the most important harvest from the sea was salt (see
Chapter 3), but seaweed and coastal vegetables such as samphire (*Salicornia
europaea* etc. and *Crithmum maritimum*) and scurvy-grass (*Cochlearia anglica*
etc.) must have been used too when and where they were available.
Coastal grazing must have been exploited too, as by the North Ronaldsay
sheep of today.[31] Such traditions, even more local and seasonal than those
concerning fish, have left few records. Although we have been able to
deduce some regional variations in Anglo-Saxon diet (between north and
south, or coast and inland), there must have been a whole texture of much
smaller-scale differences, the result of minute variations in climate and

terrain and the fact that most people did not buy their food, even from nearby, but relied on what they themselves could produce, and perhaps exchange with their neighbours. These are the kind of unconsidered trifles, a balance of seasoning, or even a fuel that gives baked goods a particular smell, that make what people eat feel like 'home' and contribute to their identity in much more subtle ways than we can hope to discern across two thousand years.

SIX

THE BEST OF FEASTS
An Anglo-Saxon Meal

The 'best of feasts' features in the great epic poem *Beowulf*. This was the ideal Anglo-Saxon meal, and yet we are not told what was eaten. We know almost as little about actual Anglo-Saxon meals. It is virtually impossible to tell what is being eaten in the few manuscript illustrations of feasts, or in the Bayeux Tapestry. There is the 'shopping list' for two funeral feasts in the Bury will fragment, but these are special meals, not what people ate every day. If a feast consisted of bread, beer and meat, with cheese, fish and milk as extras (probably for monks), what was an ordinary meal like? We can guess that it provided less meat, with dairy goods perhaps making up the deficiency, and possibly less bread as well, or if there was bread, it might not have been made of wheat. Beer might still have been drunk, or perhaps milk-derivatives. The main dish might have been a *briw* of cereals or pulses, flavoured with vegetables and maybe a bit of bacon. In fact, for 'ordinary Anglo-Saxons', this might well have been the only dish.

One feature that would have distinguished Anglo-Saxon meals quite clearly from our own is seasonality. Certain foods keep well, others can be preserved, but many would only be available in the seasons they were produced. Cereals and pulses would be available all the year round, as long as supplies did not run out before the new harvest came in. Preserved fish, cured meat and hard cheese might be available at any time of year. For a special occasion, animals could presumably be slaughtered whatever the season. For instance, the Bury funeral feast cannot have taken place during the winter, since fresh milk was available, but as well as bacon, pork, beef and venison were to be served. Some vegetables would grow through most of the winter, notably leeks and some kinds of cabbage. Onions and garlic would be in store. But most vegetables would be eaten fresh in the summer and autumn. Most of them would have had shorter seasons than now, since extended availability has been one of the main goals of vegetable breeding. In the spring there would have been a reliance on wild biennials and perennials. Cabbages may have been over-wintered. But the shortage of vegetables, and possibly even cereals, in the spring and early summer would be made up for by the abundance of milk and products like fresh cheese, butter and whey or buttermilk. Late summer and autumn would be the season of plenty, with the newly harvested cereals and pulses, and the greatest abundance of fresh vegetables. In the winter more meat might be eaten because there was less of everything else to go with the bread. Fat pigs and geese would be ready for slaughter. By spring the over-wintered animals would be in a rather run-down condition, but soon young animals like lamb would be ready, as well as eggs.

RECIPES

Perhaps surprisingly, there are some recipes surviving from Anglo-Saxon England. There are no English cook-books earlier than the fourteenth century,[1] but the Old English medical collections contain not only recipes for medicines, but also recommendations for patients' diet, including a few recipes, some of which have been quoted already. Most of these are for some kind of soup or stew, that is to say in Anglo-Saxon terms a *briw*, but that may be because this is invalid food, easy to digest. The recommendations include things like 'foods that have cooling and strengthening virtues, such as apples, not too sweet at all, but sour–sweet, and pears and peaches, and bread put in cold water or hot', or 'the meat of small animals, and little birds boiled and roasted, and various kinds of apples, pears and medlars, peas thinned down and boiled in water and in vinegar, or in wine, good and sweet'.[2] Some of these items, boiled peas, or bread in water, almost amount to cooking instructions. As well as the 'broth of mint or carrot/parsnip or cumin or ginger' already mentioned, there are lists like 'thin broth and juicy peas and beaten eggs and bread crumbled into hot water and shelled winkles with peas' or 'juicy peas and bread in hot water and oxymel (vinegar-and-honey) … celery boiled in water'.[3] In both these lists it is hard to know where one 'item' ends and another begins, but at least the methods of preparation are reasonably clear.

The beaten eggs mentioned above may be scrambled, and there is another instance of scrambled eggs or an omelette: 'then beat in butter, lay in oil, then put over the fire for a while'.[4] One recipe calls for 'clean new butter and new barley meal or grits/groats made into a *briw* together as cooks know how'.[5] The implication is that the physician need not bother preparing this himself because ordinary domestic skills will suffice. This list finishes up with 'juice (or soup?) of peas with plantain and liquid honey', and another also has the juice or soup of peas with honey, but whether such combinations were popular with healthy people it is hard to know.[6] Pea broth with vinegar sounds more familiar.[7] This appears in a passage that also recommends garlic in chicken broth, leek boiled with plantain, and mature cheese boiled in goat's milk with goat fat. Another one has shellfish in soup.[8]

Boiled vegetables are recommended for invalids: 'Give him the foods that are easy to digest. That is boiled vegetables … add a little salt and oil and celery, and leek and similar things.'[9] Elsewhere we find boiled cabbage in good broth, and instructions to simmer beet in butter, or 'boil celery and fennel, make a good broth, or juice, and of other sweet plants'.[10]

Readers might want to try some of these combinations in a recreated meal, to give some relief from the rather plain fare of meat and cereals that the Anglo-Saxons liked. On the other hand, if plantain and honey with peas sounds unappetising, remember this is invalid food. There is no need for healthy people to eat it.

COOKING METHODS

Ælfric's *Colloquy* refers to roasting that which is to be roasted, and boiling that which is to be boiled.[11] The reference to roasting shows that he is thinking primarily of meat, the centrepiece of any meal that was at all cel-ebratory. St Cuthbert boiled a goose when he had visitors.[12] Large pieces of meat may have been roasted outdoors, rather than at the domestic hearth. There is no evidence for the cooking of whole or half animals (not large ones like pigs or oxen, anyway), and it is much easier to make sure the meat is properly cooked if it is in smaller pieces. There are also no medieval recipes for boiling or roasting meat. Cooks are assumed to understand such 'plain cooking' – it is the trimmings they need instruc-tions for, and these developed after our period. It has also been suggested that food, again presumably meat, was baked in underground pits with hot stones in the early period.[13] There are no references to anything other than bread being cooked in ovens, but they could also have been used to bake meat, and the residual heat after the loaves came out could be used for drying or even for slow cooking, for instance of a stew in a pot. The recipes quoted above involve boiling and frying, and nearly all cooking must have been done on the kitchen fire (the only fire in most households).

MEALTIMES

The food rent paid to the king is called in Domesday Book *firma unius noctis*, the 'farm of one night'.[14] Originally, when the king literally travelled around his properties eating up his food rents, he must have travelled during the day, arriving towards evening, then dined, spent the night, and moved on the next day, presumably after some kind of breakfast. The royal household may therefore have taken its main meal fairly late, possibly after dark even in the summer. For those who could not afford lighting, however, and this would have been most Anglo-Saxons, it was necessary either to eat in daylight or by firelight. In the busiest periods of the year, people may have eaten something out in the fields during the day, and then had their main meal when they got home at night. In the winter, however, when they may have been engaged on indoor tasks, the main meal might have been earlier, possibly before dark. Cooking at least would need to be done in reasonable light, to make sure the food was sufficiently cooked, and would not make people ill.

An early main meal in the winter, but a later one, with an extra meal fitted in during the day, in the summer, is also found in the monastic *horarium*. In the winter the monks ate *ad nonam* (3 p.m.), whereas in the summer their *prandium* was usually *ad sextam* (at midday), and their *cena ad uesperam* (in the evening).[15] These times were varied by fast and feast-days, but, even so, monks' lives had to be much more regular than those of the laity. Nevertheless, this general pattern of eating in the afternoon in winter, but at noon and evening in summer, may have corresponded with secular expectations. Not only is the day longer in the summer than in the winter, but there was more work to be done in those longer days, and thus people needed more energy. In hot weather they would also need to stop fairly frequently for a drink, to avoid dehydration, and thus summer breaks may have been less formal and more numerous than the monastic *prandium*. In the winter, on the other hand, they would need more calories to keep up their body heat. To some extent working, warmer clothes, the fire or staying in bed would keep people warm, but they would also need foods high in carbohydrates and fat, such as a *briw* based on cereal or pulses, with some bacon or lard added.

Presumably the main cooking would be done for the main meal. Porridge can be produced quite quickly by boiling up oatmeal soaked overnight, but otherwise breakfast, if any, might consist of bread or last night's leftovers. It would certainly make sense to use them up as soon as possible. A hot breakfast might be welcome in the winter, but otherwise I am assuming that any morning meal was informal, taken as and when people felt the need. In the summer, if people got up before dawn, they might break their fast at their first break in the fields. The food taken out to work in the summer would need to be already prepared and easily transported. Bread, cheese and beer seem obvious choices.[16] In the longest days, the women would be able to spend part of the day in the fields before coming home to cook the evening meal. If even that consisted of cold food, they might only have to take one day off a week to bake bread and perhaps make cheese (not Sunday, however, as baking counted as work and was therefore forbidden).[17]

CHOOSING INGREDIENTS

Our recreated meal then will be a main meal, as everything else was probably rather casual. To be really authentic, we ought to eat it around dusk, but any time in the evening will do. In fact, to be really authentic we ought to grow almost everything ourselves, thresh and winnow our own corn, perhaps parch it too, and then kneel at the quern to grind it.[18] But there is no need to go to extremes; the results will be quite convincing if we start with ingredients from the shops. You might want to choose stone-ground flour, for its texture, or avoid carrots, since only the wrong colour will be available. You should be able to find field beans in whole-food stores, or try Egyptian *ful mesdames*, which are midway between field and broad beans. Most of the vegetables – leeks, onions, kale – will be at your local market, or you could gather fat hen from the wild. You could try to find meat from unimproved breeds, but it will not make too much difference if you have to make do with modern ones. Look out for local fruit that is in season, rather than strawberries at Christmas. In fact, it would be a good idea in general to choose foods in season, unless you want to recreate a Christmas feast in the summer, for instance. Choose your ingredients to suit the time of year, how special an occasion you want it to be, and even what social class you want to emulate. But perhaps no-one would want to eat like an Anglo-Saxon peasant.

SERVING

There would be no courses in the modern sense; when menus first appear in the fourteenth century, each course is like a meal in itself, with meat as a centrepiece, plus cereals, vegetables and fruit. By that period there were also sweet dishes and 'subtleties'.[19] But all this elaboration was a post-Conquest development. In our period, everything would be served at once. The 'best' food, the meat, might be placed in front of the guest of honour. People would bring their own knives, and probably drinking vessels. They might have their own bowls (probably wooden) and spoons (horn or wood) as well. Boiled food would be served from the cooking vessel (ceramic or iron), roast meat perhaps on a platter. Plates probably didn't exist. Fruit, cheese, and anything else without too much juice would be eaten from the hand. Meat might be placed on bread to catch the juices, but there is no evidence for coarse bread being made especially for such 'trenchers' as in the later Middle Ages.[20] We know very little about food vessels, because drinking ones were more important. For a feast, perhaps the lady of the house should take the drinking horn round to the 'heroes'. For a less fancy meal you might want to stick to your own.

~ *Menu Suggestions* ~

Select from the following: more items for a fancy meal, fewer for a plainer one. Apart from the drink, they are in something like the Anglo-Saxon order of preference, so choose more from the top of the list for a feast, more from the bottom for everyday.

Meat: beef, mutton, goose or pork in the winter, and also game; lamb or kid in spring and summer; bacon or poultry all the year round; boiled or roast; more than one item for a special meal, especially in the winter.

Fish: fresh if you live near the sea or a river, salt cod or herring otherwise; shellfish in the winter.

Cheese: hard cheese at any time, fresh cheeses in spring and summer.

Bread: made of sifted wheat for a feast, wholemeal or even barley for an ordinary meal; serve with butter or fresh cheese in spring and summer, otherwise lard.

Fruit and nuts: apples or pears from August through to December, soft fruit in the summer; you could serve it with cream in the summer, although not strictly authentic; hazelnuts in autumn and winter.

A cereal *briw*: based on barley or oats, perhaps wheat or rye, flavoured with leeks, onions, garlic or cabbage in the winter, wild herbs in the spring, onions, garlic, cabbage, beets etc. in summer and autumn; bacon at any time; cook over a slow fire (or in a slow oven, although there is not much evidence for this).

Pulses: dried peas or beans flavoured and cooked as above; mainly a winter dish.

Fresh vegetables: peas, beans, cabbage, beets etc. in season; tender vegetables like spring onions might be served raw; use up any gluts in the garden (if of appropriate vegetables); mainly a summer dish.

Drink: wine, mead and beer, probably in that order of desirability, are in season all year; no particular wine has been produced continuously since the early Middle Ages, but a sweet one might be appropriate; choose ale rather than lager; avoid 'mead' based on grapes, and only flavoured with honey; milk, buttermilk or water (or even whey if you can get it) for children and monks.

God lif!

END NOTES

Introduction

1 On feasting in Anglo-Saxon England, see Hugh Magennis's two books, *Anglo-Saxon Appetites* and *Images of Community*, and also Marjorie A. Brown, 'The Feast Hall'.
2 The lists of food for the funeral feasts are in a fragmentary will edited by Robertson, *Charters*, p.252.
3 The first two are edited by Liebermann, *Gesetze*, pp.444–53 and 453–5, respectively, the last by Robertson, *Charters*, 252–6.
4 Edited by Garmonsway, *Colloquy*.
5 The *Indicia* is edited and translated in Banham, *Indicia*.
6 The first two are edited by Cockayne, *Leechdoms* vol. II, and the last by Pettit, *Anglo-Saxon Remedies*. *Leechbook III* is so called because it used to be thought part of *Bald's Leechbook*. For more on all these texts, see Cameron, *Anglo-Saxon Medicine*.
7 See Keynes and Lapidge, *Alfred the Great*, pp.197–202.
8 See Morris, *Craft, Industry and Everyday Life*.
9 For a summary of this evidence, see Payne, 'Animal Husbandry'.
10 The archaeobotanical records in this book are drawn from my thesis, 'Food Plants', supplemented by information from Hagen, *Second Handbook*. Further data are available in the Archaeobotanical Computer Database – see Tomlinson and Hall, *ABCD*.
11 An excellent introduction to English place-names and their uses is Gelling, *Signposts to the Past*.
12 On the Old English language, see Mitchell and Robinson, *Guide to Old English*.
13 For Anglo-Saxon art in general, and a huge compendium of illustrations, see Wilson, *Anglo-Saxon Art*.
14 See the facsimile edition by D'Aronco and Cameron.

Chapter 1

1 See for instance Feldman, Lupton and Miller, 'Wheats', p.184.
2 The archaeological data in this chapter come from my thesis, Banham, 'Food Plants', chapter 2, supplemented by Hagen, *Second Handbook*, chapter 1, and later work.
3 See Petra Dark, *Environment*, p. 27, for climatic trends.
4 I have followed the taxonomy given by the authors of the relevant articles in Smartt and Simmonds, *Evolution of Crop Plants*.

5 Huntley, 'Saxon-Norse Economy'.
6 Hugh Thomas, 'Oats', p.132.
7 Regional variations like this are much more apparent after the Anglo-Saxon period, and their development can be traced in the volumes of *The Agrarian History of England and Wales*, ed. H.P.R. Finberg and Joan Thirsk.
8 Emiko Ohnuki-Tierney, *Rice as Self*, p.42.
9 Robertson, *Charters*, pp.252–3. The will is undated, but certainly late – see Robertson's notes on p.501.
10 For instance in the extensive eleventh-century account of Bury food rents etc. edited by Robertson, *Charters*, pp.192–201.
11 It occurs only in the Laws of King Æthelberht of Kent, Liebermann, *Gesetze* I, p.4.
12 Liebermann, *Gesetze* I, p.3.
13 For the distribution of mills in 1086, see Darby, *Domesday Geography*, pp.270–5. Windmills did not come in until the twelfth century, but there were also tidal mills and those driven by oxen.
14 See Banham, 'Food Plants', pp.77–9, for some instances.
15 Dobbie, *Minor Poems*, p.205.
16 Sawyer no.1239, edited in Kelly, *St Augustine's*, no.25.
17 Banham, 'Food Plants', pp.72–4.
18 One is in the anonymous *Historia abbatum* of Wearmouth and Jarrow, edited in Plummer, *Bedae opera historica*, p.389, and the other in the anonymous Life of St Cuthbert, edited by Colgrave in *Two Lives*, p.78.
19 Hagen, *Handbook*, p.3, suggests they may have been used for more than one purpose, which seems likely. The classic discussion of these structures is Monk, 'Post-Roman Drying Kilns'. For a pre-AD 800 building and oven identified by the excavators as a bake-house, see Wade-Martins, *North Elmham Park*, vol. 1, pp.69–73. This was probably an episcopal establishment.
20 See under 'Bread' in Davidson, *Companion*.
21 *ibid*.
22 Hagen, *Handbook*, p.10, lists some possible commercial ovens and bakeries from Domesday Book, but they are all urban. David, *English Bread*, p.161, quotes Eliza Acton's 1857 statement that 'not only are there no ovens in vast numbers of our cottages, but many a small village is entirely without one.'
23 Keith Wade, personal communication.
24 Murphy, *Buttermarket*, quoted by permission of Peter Murphy.
25 Chris Wickham, personal communication.
26 For instance in a lease to Bishop Denewulf of Winchester, possibly of AD 909, Robertson, *Charters*, p.39.
27 This is the *Æcerbot* charm, Dobbie, *Minor Poems*, p.118.
28 Hagen, *Second Handbook*, lists the archaeological finds at pp.27–8.
29 Matthew ch. 13 vv.24–30.
30 Forsyth, *Poisonous Plants*, p.47.
31 Glasswell, *The Earliest English*, p.65.
32 See Mason and Brown, *Traditional Foods*, pp.55–6.
33 See Heiatt and Butler, *Curye on Inglysch*, e.g. pp.98–9.
34 Hagen lists a number of these, *Second Handbook*, pp.212–14.
35 *Bald's Leechbook* II.51, Cockayne II, p.268.
36 Peter Murphy, personal communication.
37 See Wilson, 'Graveney Boat'.

38 Peter Murphy, personal communication.
39 *Bald's Leechbook* II.51, para. 1, Cockayne II, pp.264–6.
40 Quoted by Grigson, *Englishman's Flora*, p.240.
41 Glover, *Encyclopedia of Beer*, p.15.
42 See Seymour, *Self-Sufficiency*, p.158. This is not of course the 'fresh' yeast now sold by health-food shops and bakers, which is compressed and refrigerated. Fresh yeast is a frothy liquid.
43 Liebermann, *Gesetze* I, pp.118–21.
44 *Leechbook* III.30, Cockayne II, p.324.
45 Sawyer nos 146 and 1440, edited by Birch, *Cartularium Saxonicum*, no.273 and Robertson, *Charters*, p.12, respectively.
46 I.67, para. 1, item 2, Cockayne II, p.142.
47 For example, *Bald's Leechbook* I.37, para. 2, Cockayne II, p.90.
48 These questions are discussed at greater length at Banham, 'Plant Foods', pp.101–2.
49 *Images of Community*, and *Anglo-Saxon Appetites*, especially pp.21–8.

Chapter 2
1 Hagen lists them in *Handbook*, Appendix D, pp.151–4.
2 For all you ever wanted to know on the Faba bean, see Hebblethwaite, *Faba Bean*.
3 See for instance Heiatt and Butler, *Curye on Inglysch*, p.98.
4 *Bald's Leechbook* II.24, Cockayne II, p.214.
5 Liebermann, *Gesetze* I, p.450. The ration for male slaves differs considerably, but is not clear what lies behind these differences.
6 Signs 62 and 63, Banham, *Indicia*, pp.32–3.
7 See Banham, 'Food Plants', p.176, for a more extended discussion of this.
8 Wilson, *Food and Drink in Britain*, p.206.
9 See Banham, 'Food Plants', p.195.
10 For which see Fenton, *Scottish Country Life*, pp.178–9.
11 This extensive and complex vocabulary is discussed in Banham, 'Food Plants', pp.182–94.
12 Sign 59, Banham, *Indicia*, pp.32–3.
13 Colgrave, *Two Lives*, p.276.
14 Krapp and Dobbie, *Exeter Book*, p.193. The other two riddles referred to are at pp.238 and 230 respectively.
15 I.2, item 7, Cockayne II, p.26. The most common foods are often alleged to be hard to digest in medieval medicine.
16 Clapham, Tutin and Moore, *Flora*, p.71.
17 Hodgkin, 'Cabbages', p.77.
18 In *Bald's Leechbook* I.33, item 3 (Cockayne II, p.80), and Wellcome MS46, a short medical collection, (Napier, 'Altenglische Miscellen', p.326), respectively.
19 Mabey, *Food for Free*, p.103.
20 Fenton, *Scottish Country Life*, p.169.
21 Hogkin, 'Cabbages', p.79.
22 For the Anglo-Saxon terminology, see Banham, 'Food Plants' pp.201–2. I hope to explore this more fully in a future publication under the auspices of the Anglo-Saxon Plant-Names Survey, Department of English Language, University of Glasgow.
23 I follow the terminology of MacNaughton, 'Turnips and Relatives' and 'Swedes and Rapes', in Smartt and Simmonds, *Crop Plants*, pp.62–8 and 68–75 respectively.
24 Ford-Lloyd, 'Sugarbeet, and other Cultivated Beets', p.36.

25 This is assembled in Banham, 'Food Plants', pp.203–6.

26 Clapham, Tutin and Moore, *Flora*, p.159.

27 *Bald's Leechbook* II.33, para. 2, item 13, Cockayne II, p.238.

28 Ford-Lloyd, 'Sugarbeet, and other Cultivated Beets', p.35.

29 The terminology is discussed in Banham, 'Food Plants', pp.196–9.

30 Riggs, 'Carrot', p.478.

31 Clapham, Tutin and Moore, *Flora*, p.294. See Vaughan and Geissler, *Food Plants*, p.84, for a description of the wild form.

32 Recent work on the history of carrot breeding is summarised in Riggs, 'Carrot'.

33 Riggs, 'Umbelliferous Minor Crops', p.482.

34 See Vaughan and Geissler, *Food Plants*, p.185, for illustrations by B.E. Nicholson. These show the cultivated plants, but their above-ground parts have not been subject to much human selection.

35 See Alcock, *Food in Roman Britain*, p.63.

36 cf. Vaughan and Geissler, *Food Plants*, p.184, and Clapham, Tutin and Moore, *Flora*, p.292.

37 *Bald's Leechbook* I.18, item 10, Cockayne II, p.62.

38 The vocabulary is discussed in Banham, 'Food Plants', pp.206–8.

39 Crisp, 'Radish', p.87.

40 The prescription is against heart pain, I.17, para. 2, Cockayne II, p.60.

41 Listed in Banham, 'Food Plants', pp.207–8.

42 *Lacnunga* 125 and 178, Pettit, *Anglo-Saxon Remedies*, pp.88 and 122, respectively.

43 These names are discussed in Banham, 'Food Plants', pp.211–14.

44 *ibid.*, pp.213–14.

45 Clapham, Tutin and Moore, *Flora*, pp.99–100.

46 Godden, *Catholic Homilies*, p.158.

47 Collected at Banham, 'Food Plants', pp.222–6.

48 See Mabey, *Food for Free*, pp.89–90.

49 See under 'Spinach' in Davidson, *Companion*.

50 The late Peter Reynolds thought it likely they were eaten in the Iron Age: *Iron-Age Farm*, p.67.

51 The exception to this would be religious communities. The *Indicia* gives signs for both raw and boiled vegetables, following the Benedictine Rule: signs 57 and 58, Banham, *Indicia*, pp.32–3.

52 Riggs, 'Umbelliferous Minor Crops', p.482.

53 See Wren, *Potter's Cyclopaedia, sub verbo*, for medical uses.

54 Listed at Banham, 'Food Plants', pp.226–8. The *briw* recipe is *Bald's Leechbook* II.51, para. 1, item 3, Cockayne II, p.264.

55 See Banham, 'Food Plants', p.228.

56 *Bald's Leechbook* II.30, item 2, Cockayne II, p.226. The other instances are listed at Banham, 'Food Plants', pp.229–31.

57 Clapham, Tutin and Moore, *Flora*, p.286.

58 Banham, 'Food Plants', pp.231–3.

59 *Bald's Leechbook* I.18, item 10, Cockayne II, p.62.

60 Banham, 'Food Plants', pp.236–43.

61 *Bald's Leechbook* II.39, item 5, Cockayne II, p.248.

62 *Bald's Leechbook* I.48, para. 1, item 2, Cockayne II, p.120.

63 Garmonsway, *Colloquy*, p.33.

64 See Davidson, *Companion*, under 'Pepper'.

65 Alcock, *Roman Britain*, p.71.

66 Colgrave and Mynors, *Ecclesiastical History*, p.584; Tangl, *Briefen*, p.80.

67 Sign 61, Banham, *Indicia*, pp.32–3.

68 Wellcome MS 46, Napier, 'Altenglische Miscellen', p.326.

69 See Banham, 'Food Plants', pp.245–50.

70 e.g. *Bald's Leechbook* II.16, Cockayne II, p.94.

71 Sign 86, Banham, *Indicia*, pp.38–9.

72 *ibid.*, pp.75–6.

73 See Davidson, *Companion*, under 'Mustard'.

74 See Banham 'Food Plants', p.248.

75 For general discussion of dietary salt, see Davidson, *Companion*, under 'Salt'.

76 See Hagen, *Handbook*, pp.40–1, for some examples.

77 Alcock, *Roman Britain*, pp.73–5.

78 Anglo-Saxon salt production is summarised in Hagen, *Handbook*, p.40.

79 Hagen lists some of the documentation in *ibid.*, p.41.

80 Garmonsway, *Colloquy*, pp.35–6.

81 Some medical instances are listed by Hagen, *Handbook*, at p.36.

82 Sign no. 68, Banham, *Indicia*, pp.34–5.

83 See Paston-Williams, *Art of Dining*, p.74 and illustration on p.37.

84 For a huge compendium of information, much of it historical, about honey, see Crane, *Honey*.

85 Sign 69, Banham, *Indicia*, pp.34–5.

86 II.26 and 37, Cockayne II, pp.220 and 246.

87 e.g. *Bald's Leechbook* I.1, para. 17, item 3, Cockayne II, p.25.

88 Hagen lists several in *Second Handbook*, pp.153 and 157–8.

89 Some of them are listed by Hagen, *Second Handbook*, pp.150–1 and 154–5.

90 Liebermann, *Gesetze* I, p.447.

91 Sawyer no. 1188, edited by Harmer, *Documents*, pp.1–2.

92 For the central place of drinking in Anglo-Saxon feasts, see Magennis, *Anglo-Saxon Appetites*, pp. 21–8, and for the absence of references to food, *ibid.*, pp.29–36.

93 Edited by Lapidge and Winterbottom, *Life of St Æthelwold*. This is also their translation.

Chapter 3

1 Clapham, Tutin and Moore, *Flora*, pp.244, 243–4, 231, 232, 217, 206, 207–12, 257 and 256 respectively.

2 Watkins, 'Apple and Pear', pp.419–20.

3 The references suggesting cultivation in Anglo-Saxon England are collected together in Banham, 'Food Plants', pp.111–13; the last reference is from *Bald's Leechbook*, II.2, para. 2, item 1, Cockayne II, p.180.

4 The *Capitulare de uillis* is edited in Boretius, *Capitularia* I, with the list of apple varieties at p.90.

5 Morgan and Richards, *Book of Apples*, pp.199–200.

6 Morgan and Richards, *Apples*, pp.25–6.

7 Edited by Liebermann, *Gesetze*, I, pp.453–5.

8 Colloquies 25 and 28, Gwara and Porter, *Conversations*, pp.154–5 and 164–5 respectively. Although Bata's lists of trees and plants are lifted from the *Glossary* of his teacher Abbot Ælfric, there is no reason why he should have invented the idea of monasteries having orchards.

9 Banham, 'Food Plants', p.110.

10 The suggestion is M.A. Monk's, in his dissertation 'The Plant Economy'.

11 The expression occurs in the 'Nine Herbs Charm' in the *Lacnunga*, Pettit *Anglo-Saxon Remedies*, p.68. This charm is archaic in various ways, and cultivated apples may be avoided deliberately.

12 Clapham, Tutin and Moore, *Flora*, pp.243–4.

13 Watkins, 'Apple and Pear', p.420.

14 Sign no.74, Banham, *Indicia*, pp.34–5.

15 Watkins, 'Cherry, plum', pp.424–5.

16 The references, such as they are, are collected in Banham, 'Food Plants', pp.122–3.

17 Sign no.74, Banham, *Indicia*, pp.34–5; Zupitza, *Grammatik und Glossar*, p.20.

18 The evidence is given in Banham, 'Food Plants', p.123; sign no.76, Banham, *Indicia*, pp.36–7.

19 Mabey, *Food for Free*, p.171.

20 The archaeological finds are listed in Banham, 'Food Plants', p.126.

21 Banham, 'Food Plants', pp.124–5.

22 *ibid.*, pp.126–7 and 129–30.

23 e.g. *Lacnunga* 14, Pettit, *Anglo-Saxon Remedies*, p.8.

24 Elizabeth Keep, 'Currants', in Smartt and Simmonds, pp.235–9, at p.236, and Mason and Brown, *Traditional Foods*, p.33.

25 *Lacnunga* 133, Pettit, *Anglo-Saxon Remedies*, p.96.

26 See Banham, 'Food Plants', pp.124, 117–8 and 134 respectively.

27 The finds are listed at Banham, 'Food Plants', p.153.

28 I.1, Colgrave and Mynors, p.14.

29 The evidence is given in Banham, 'Food Plants', pp.143–5. For climate, see Dark, *The Environment*, pp.27–8.

30 Liebermann, *Gesetze*, p.154; Darby, *Domesday England*, pp.275–7 and 362–3.

31 Letter 8, Dümmler II, p.33.

32 Lines 1232–3, Klaeber, p.47.

33 Garmonsway, *Colloquy*, p.47.

34 Banham, *Indicia*, pp.26–7 and 62–3.

35 Signs 84 and 86, Banham, *op. cit.*, pp.36–9.

36 Alcock, *Roman Britain*, pp.85–7.

37 Fell, 'Old English *beor*'.

38 Sign no.85, Banham, *op. cit.*, pp.38–9.

39 For some examples, see Banham and Mason, 'Confectionery Recipes'.

40 Listed in Banham, 'Food Plants', pp.156–7.

41 Clapham, Tutin and Moore, *Flora*, p.315, Rackham, *Countryside*, pp.66ff.

42 Banham, 'Food Plants', pp.161–4.

43 *ibid.*, pp.158–9.

44 B. Ibbs, personal communication.

45 Banham, 'Food Plants', pp.159–60.

46 *ibid.*, pp.160–1.

47 There are many such recipes in Heiatt and Butler, *Curye on Inglysch*.

48 Mabey, *Food for Free*, p.29.

Chapter 4

1 Roberts, 'Malnutrition', p.299.

2 *ibid.*

3 See Hagen, *Handbook*, Appendix D.

4 Garmonsway, *Colloquy*, p.22.

5 Liebermann, *Gesetze* I, pp.451.

6 The present-day proportions are about 4:2:1. Yields for cows and goats are given by Mackenzie, *Goat Husbandry*, p.25, and for sheep by Alderson, *Chance to Survive*, p.57. These are figures per animal, not per acre or per kilo of fodder.

7 Kelly, *Early Irish Farming*, p.52.

8 Liebermann, *Gesetze* I, pp.451.

9 Contemporary Irish sources regard summer and autumn as the milking season, according to Kelly, *Early Irish Farming*, p.52.

10 Ryder, *Sheep and Man*, p.721.

11 *De temporum ratione* 15, Wallis, *The Reckoning of Time*, pp.53–4.

12 Sign no.66, Banham, *Indicia*, pp.34–5.

13 The quotation from John Skene of Hallyards is given by Fenton, 'Milk products', p.43.

14 Originally it may have been ease of transport that was more important, but by the end of the period most of the food may have gone into long-term storage.

15 Sign no.64, Banham, *Indicia*, pp.34–5.

16 Sign no.65, Banham, *Indicia*, pp.34–5.

17 IV Æthelred, Liebermann, *Gesetze* I, p.232.

18 Gísladóttir, 'Whey', p.125.

19 Fenton, *Northern Isles*, p.443.

20 Garmonsway, *Colloquy*, p.47.

21 Gísladóttir, 'Whey', pp.126–7.

22 Fenton, *Northern Isles*, pp.442–3, Gísladóttir, 'Whey', pp.122–3, 127.

23 Clayton, 'Common Duck', pp.335–6, suggests the twelfth century. Harper, 'Tardy Domestication', p.389, presents some ninth-century Frankish evidence for the classification of ducks with domestic poultry, but this may not be relevant to Britain. Kelly, *Early Irish Farming*, p.107, found few references to ducks in early medieval Irish sources.

24 Garmonsway, *Colloquy*, p.31.

25 II.56, Cockayne II, p.278.

26 Fenton, *Northern Isles*, pp.513–15 and 519–21.

27 II.49, Cockayne II, p.264.

28 Sign no.67, Banham, *Indicia*, pp.34–5. See also the note on p.71.

29 Bond, 'Hunting', p.244, gives several references to the hunting activities of kings and one bishop, and to lands granted to huntsmen. *Rectitudines* refers to the duty of maintaining the king's hunting enclosure.

30 Latin *dama*, but it is doubtful whether fallow deer were introduced into Britain before the Norman Conquest.

31 Garmonsway, *Colloquy*, p.24.

32 The archaeological remains are summarised by Bond, 'Hunting', p.244.

33 Payne, 'Animal Husbandry', p.39.

34 Some examples are listed at Banham, 'Food Plants', pp.161–2.

35 Darby, *Domesday England*, p.171.

36 An example is Sawyer no.1493, printed by Kemble, *Codex Diplomaticus*, no.971.

37 Pheifer, *Épinal–Erfurt*, p.32.

38 This occurs in a list of Bishop Æthelwold's gifts to Peterborough, from the Peterborough Cartulary, edited by Robertson, *Charters*, p.74.

39 This seems to be the only instance of *smea* as a simplex, but in compounds it means penetrating, and then by extension profound, sophisticated, ingenious.

40 Garmonsway, *Colloquy*, p.46.
41 Sign 78, Banham, *Indicia*, pp.36–7.
42 Knowles, *Monastic Order*, p.461.
43 *De temporum ratione* 15, Wallis, *The Reckoning of Time*, pp.53–4.
44 This archaeo-osteological evidence is summarised by Payne, 'Animal Husbandry', p.39.
45 Payne, p.39, gives figures of 100–130cm at the shoulder for cattle, 50–70cm for sheep.
46 For an example see Alderson, *Chance to Survive*, pp.62 and 155.
47 Knowles, *Monastic Order*, p.458.
48 Item 14, Grant, *Anthimus*, pp.54–7.
49 For the development of modern breeds, see Epstein and Bichard, 'Pig', pp.151–2. A slightly different account is given by Alderson, *Chance to Survive*, pp.41–3, and on pp.61–2 he discusses renewed interest in the leaner 'unimproved' breeds at the present day.
50 Lines 48–50, Ehwald, *Opera omnia*, pp.147–8.
51 Cobbett, *Cottage Economy*, pp.129–30. See Mason, 'Lard' for traditional uses in Britain, Europe and further afield.

Chapter 5
1 See the recent study by Alison Locker, The *Role of Stored Fish in England 900–1750 AD*.
2 See Fenton, *Northern Isles*, p.531, for an example.
3 See e.g. *ibid.*, p.613.
4 Translation based on Magennis, *Anglo-Saxon Appetites*, p.91, from text edited by Dobbie, *The Anglo-Saxon Minor Poems*, p.104, amended by Magennis, p.90.
5 They feature under 'Economical Cookery' in my 1900 Mrs Beeton, page c.
6 Krapp and Dobbie, *Exeter Book*, p.234.
7 Signs 70–2, Banham, *Indicia*, pp.34–5.
8 Garmonsway, *Colloquy*, p.29.
9 *Bald's Leechbook* II. 49 and 27, respectively, Cockayne II, pp.264 and 222.
10 *ibid.*, pp.27–8. I reproduce the Latin, for anyone who would like to attempt their own translation: Anguillas et lucios, menas et capitones, tructas et murenas, et qualescumque in amne natant. Saliu. (This last word might be something to do with salt, *sal*, but it is glossed by OE *sprote*, sprat.)
11 In this they have the support of the present-day authority, Alan Davidson, who censures Roman and modern writers for 'undue emphasis on the merits of this or that particular species'. See Davidson, *Companion*, under 'Fish'.
12 Crabtree, *West Stow*, p.106.
13 Some Domesday fishponds are listed by Hagen, *Second Handbook*, pp.163–4.
14 See Salisbury, 'Fishweirs', for the archaeological evidence.
15 See Faith, 'Tidenham', p.44.
16 Garmonsway, *Colloquy*, p.29.
17 IV Æthelræd, Liebermann, *Gesetze* I, p.232.
18 Garmonsway, *Colloquy*, p.30.
19 Godden, 'Ælfric', p.8.
20 Garmonsway, *Colloquy*, p.27.
21 Locker, *Stored Fish*, pp.277–8.
22 IV Æthelræd, Liebermann, *Gesetze* I, p.232.
23 Robertson, *Charters*, p.252.
24 Garmonsway, *Colloquy*, pp.35–6. See Hagen, *Handbook*, pp.34–6 and 39–42, for Anglo-Saxon salt and salting.

25 See Locker pp.51–8 for all these methods of preservation as they affect fish. For domestic drying and smoking in Scotland, see Fenton, *Scottish Country Life*, pp.175–6.
26 Not that this means the legends about their origins are true. See Mason and Brown, *Traditional Foods*, pp.81–4 and 104 respectively.
27 Locker, p.44. None of the evidence is Anglo-Saxon, unfortunately.
28 Locker, p.50, explains that there is little archaeological evidence for salmon as its bones perish easily. Eel do not figure in her data either as they were apparently not a commercial species.
29 See Darby, *Domesday England*, pp.283–4 for some examples.
30 For instance Robertson, *Charters*, pp.100 and 170.
31 Alderson, *Chance to Survive*, pp.64–6.

Chapter 6
1 The earliest ones are edited by Heiatt and Butler, *Curye on Inglysch*.
2 *Bald's Leechbook* II.1 and 2 respectively, Cockayne II, pp.176 and 180.
3 *ibid.*, II.49 and 43 respectively, Cockayne II, pp.264 and 254.
4 *Lacnunga* 398, Pettit, *Anglo-Saxon Remedies* I, p.22.
5 *Bald's Leechbook* II.26, Cockayne II, pp.220.
6 The second one is from *Bald's Leechbook* II.37, Cockayne II, p.226.
7 *Bald's Leechbook* II.56, Cockayne II, pp.278.
8 *Bald's Leechbook* II. 27, Cockayne II, pp.222.
9 British Library MS Harley 55, fo. 1 recto, para. 9, Cockayne II, pp.282.
10 *Leechbook III*, chapter 12, Cockayne II, pp.314, *Lacnunga* 56, Pettit, *Anglo-Saxon Remedies* I, p.26, and *Bald's Leechbook* II.30, item 2, Cockayne II, pp.254.
11 Garmonsway, *Colloquy*, p.37.
12 Colgrave, *Two Lives*, pp.268–9.
13 Glasswell, *The Earliest English*, p.102.
14 See Stafford, 'The Farm of One Night'.
15 These timings, based on the Benedictine Rule, come from the *Regularis concordia*, the 'Agreement on the Rule' of the late Anglo-Saxon monastic reformers. It is edited by Dom Thomas Symons, *Monastic Agreement*.
16 Perhaps unduly influenced by the modern brewery chain's idea of the 'ploughman's lunch'.
17 Other things forbidden by the Sunday Letter include cutting one's hair, shaving, or taking a bath; Napier, *Wulfstan*, p.212.
18 In the Northern Isles, where querns were in use until recently, they were mounted on wooden shelves, but there is no evidence for such structures in Anglo-Saxon England. In Turkey and India, women kneel, or sit with their legs stretched out on either side of the quern. See Figures 7 and 8.
19 See e.g. Heiatt and Butler, *Curye on Inglysch*, pp.39–41.
20 See Black, 'Medieval Britain', p.99.

BIBLIOGRAPHY

Ælfric, *Colloquy*, see Garmonsway.

—, *Grammar* and *Glossary*, see Zupitza.

Ælfric Bata, see Gwara and Porter.

Alcock, Joan P., *Food in Roman Britain*, Tempus 2001

Alderson, Lawrence, *The Chance to Survive*, 2nd ed. Pilkington Press 1994

Bald's Leechbook is edited in Cockayne, *Leechdoms*, vol. II.

Banham, Debby, 'The Knowledge and Uses of Food Plants in Anglo-Saxon England',
   unpublished PhD dissertation, University of Cambridge 1990

—, ed. and trans., *Monasteriales indicia: the Old English Monastic Sign Language*, Anglo-Saxon
   Books 1991

—, and Laura Mason, 'Confectionery Recipes from a Fifteenth-Century Manuscript',
   Petits Propos Culinaires 69, 2002, pp.45–69

Be gesceadwisan gerefan is edited by Liebermann, *Gesetze*, vol. I, pp.453–5.

Bede, *Ecclesiastical History*, see Colgrave and Mynors.

—, *De temporum ratione*, see Wallis.

[Beeton, Isabella], *Mrs Beeton's Family Cookery and Housekeeping Book*, Ward Lock 1900

Beowulf, see Klaeber.

Birch, W. de Gray, ed. *Cartularium Saxonicum*, 3 vols, London 1885–93

Black, Maggie, 'Medieval Britain', in *eadem*, ed., *A Taste of History: 10,000 Years of Food in
   Britain*, English Heritage/British Museum, 1993, pp.95–135

Bond, C.J., 'Hunting', in Lapidge *et al.*, *Encyclopaedia*, pp.244–5

Boretius, Alfred, *Capitularia regum Francorum*, Tomus I, Monumenta Germaniae Historica,
   Legum Sectio II, Hanover 1883

Brown, Marjorie A., 'The Feast Hall in Anglo-Saxon Society', in Martha Carlin and Joel T.
   Rosenthal, eds, *Food and Eating in Medieval Europe*, Hambledon 1998, pp.1–13

Cameron, M.L., *Anglo-Saxon Medicine*, Cambridge University Press 1993

Capitulare de uillis, see Boretius.

Clapham, A.R., T.G. Tutin and D.M. Moore, *Flora of the British Isles*, 3rd ed. Cambridge
   University Press 1987

Clayton, G.A., 'Common Duck', in Mason, *Evolution of Domesticated Animals*, pp.334–9

Cobbett, William, *Cottage Economy*, J.M. Cobbett 1823, reprinted Landsman's Bookshop
   1974

Cockayne, Rev.T.O., ed. and trans., *Leechdoms,Wortcunning and Starcraft of Early England*, 3 vols, Rolls Series 1864–6

Colgrave, Bertram, *Two Lives of St Cuthbert*, Cambridge University Press 1940

—, and R.A.B. Mynors, eds, *Bede's Ecclesiastical History of the English People*, Oxford University Press 1970

Crabtree, Pam J., *West Stow: Early Anglo-Saxon Animal Husbandry*, East Anglian Archaeology 47, Suffolk County Council 1990

Crane, Eva, *Honey: a Comprehensive Survey*, Heinemann 1975

Crisp, Peter, 'Radish', in Smartt and Simmonds, *Evolution of Crop Plants*, pp.86–9

Darby, H.C., *Domesday England*, Cambridge University Press 1977

Dark, Petra, *The Environment of Britain in the First Millennium AD*, Duckworth 2000

D'Aronco, M.A., and M.L. Cameron, eds, *The Old English Illustrated Pharmacopoeia: British Library Cotton Vitellius C III*, Early English Manuscripts in Facsimile 27, Rosenkilde and Bagger 1998

David, Elizabeth, *English Bread and Yeast Cookery*, Allen Lane 1977

Davidson, Alan, ed., *The Oxford Companion to Food*, Oxford University Press 1999

Dobbie, Elliott van Kirk, *The Anglo-Saxon Minor Poems*, Anglo-Saxon Poetic Records VI, Routledge 1942

Dümmler, Ernst, *Epistolae Karolini aeui*, Monumenta Germaniae Historica, Epistolae IV, Berlin 1895

Ehwald, R., ed., *Aldhelmi opera omnia*, Monumenta Germaniae Historica, Auctores Antiquissimi XV, Berlin 1919

Epstein, H., and M. Bichard, 'Pig', in Mason, *Evolution of Domesticated Animals*, pp.145–62

Faith, Rosamond, 'Tidenham, Gloucestershire, and the History of the Manor in England', *Landscape History* 16, 1994, pp.39–51

Feldman, Moshe, F.G.H. Lupton and T.E. Miller, 'Wheats', in Smartt and Simmonds, *Evolution of Crop Plants*, pp.184–92

Fell, Christine, 'Old English *beor*', *Leeds Studies in English* ns 8, 1975, pp.76–95

Fenton, Alexander, 'Milk Products in the Everyday Diet of Scotland', in Lysaght, *Milk and Milk Products*, pp.41–7

—, *The Northern Isles*, John Donald 1978

—, *Scottish Country Life*, John Donald 1976

Ford-Lloyd, B.V., 'Sugarbeet, and other Cultivated Beets', in Smartt and Simmonds, *Evolution of Crop Plants*, pp.35–40

Forsyth, A.A., *British Poisonous Plants*, HMSO 1968

Garmonsway, G.N., ed., *Ælfric's Colloquy*, Exeter Medieval English Texts and Studies, revised ed. 1991

Gelling, Margaret, *Signposts to the Past*, Dent 1978

Gerefa is edited by Liebermann, *Gesetze*, vol. I, pp.453–5.

Gísladóttir, Hallgerður, 'The Use of Whey in Icelandic Households', in Lysaght, *Milk and Milk Products*, pp.123–9

Glasswell, Samantha, *The Earliest English: Living and Dying in Early Anglo-Saxon England*, Tempus 2002

Glover, Brian, *The World Encyclopedia of Beer*, Anness Publishing, updated edition 1999

Godden, Malcolm, 'Ælfric of Eynsham', in Lapidge *et al.*, *Encyclopaedia*, pp.8–9

—, ed., *Ælfric's Catholic Homilies: the Second Series*, Early English Text Society ss 5, 1979

Grant, Mark, ed. and trans., *Anthimus,* De observatione ciborum*, On the Observance of Foods*, Prospect Books 1996

Grigson, Geoffrey, *The Englishman's Flora*, Phoenix House 1958

Gwara, Scott, and David W. Porter, ed. and trans., *Anglo-Saxon Conversations: the Colloquies of Ælfric Bata*, The Boydell Press 1997

Hagen, Ann, *A Handbook of Anglo-Saxon Food: Processing and Consumption*, Anglo-Saxon Books 1992

—, *A Second Handbook of Anglo-Saxon Food and Drink: Production and Distribution*, Anglo-Saxon Books 1995

Harmer, F.E., *Select English Historical Documents of the Ninth and Tenth Centuries*, Cambridge 1914

Harper, J., 'The Tardy Domestication of the Duck', *Agricultural History* 46, 1972, pp.385–9

Hebblethwaite, P.D., ed., *The Faba Bean (*Vicia faba *L.): a Basis for Improvement*, Butterworth 1983

Heiatt, Constance B., and Sharon Butler, *Curye on Inglysch: English Culinary Manuscripts of the Fourteenth Century (including the Forme of Cury)*, Early English Text Society ss 8, 1985

Hodgkin, Toby, 'Cabbages, Kales, etc.' in Smartt and Simmonds, *Evolution of Crop Plants*, pp.76–82

Huntley, Jacqueline P., 'Saxon–Norse Economy in Northern Britain: Food for Thought', *Durham Archaeological Journal* 14–15, 1999, pp.77–81

Keep, Elizabeth, 'Currants', in Smartt and Simmonds, *Evolution of Crop Plants*, pp.235–9

Kelly, Fergus, *Early Irish Farming: a Study based mainly on the Law-Texts of the 7th and 8th Centuries AD*, Dublin Institute for Advanced Studies 1997

Kelly, S.E., ed., *The Charters of St Augustine's Abbey, Canterbury*, Anglo-Saxon Charters IV, London 1994

Kemble, J.M., ed., *Codex diplomaticus aevi Saxonici*, London 1839–48

Keynes, Simon, and Michael Lapidge, *Alfred the Great: Asser's* Life of King Alfred *and other contemporary sources*, Penguin 1983

Klaeber, F., ed., *Beowulf and the Fight at Finnsburg*, 3rd ed. D. C. Heath 1950

Knowles, David, *The Monastic Order in England: a History of its Development from the Time of St Dunstan to the Fourth Lateran Council, 940–1216*, Cambridge University Press, 2nd ed. 1963

Krapp, G.P., and E. van Kirk Dobbie, eds, *The Exeter Book*, Anglo-Saxon Poetic Records III, Routledge 1936

Lapidge, Michael, *et al.*, eds, *The Blackwell Encyclopaedia of Anglo-Saxon England*, Blackwell 1999

—, and Michael Winterbottom, ed. and trans., *Wulfstan of Winchester: Life of St Æthelwold*, Clarendon Press 1991

Liebermann, F., ed., *Die Gesetze der Angelsachsen*, 3 vols, Halle 1898–1916

Locker, Alison, *The Role of Stored Fish in England 900–1750 AD: the Evidence from Historical and Archaeological Data*, Publishing Group Limited, Sofia, 2001

Lysaght, Patricia, ed., *Milk and Milk Products from Medieval to Modern Times*, Canongate 1994

Mabey, Richard, *Food for Free*, Collins 1972

Mackenzie, David, *Goat Husbandry*, Faber, 3rd ed. 1970

MacNaughton, I.H. , 'Swedes and Rapes', in Smartt and Simmonds, *Crop Plants*, pp.68–75

—, 'Turnips and Relatives', in Smartt and Simmonds, *Crop Plants*, pp.62–8

Magennis, Hugh, *Anglo-Saxon Appetites: Food and Drink and their Consumption in Old English and Related Literature*, Four Courts Press 1999

—, *Images of Community in Old English Poetry*, Cambridge Studies in Anglo-Saxon England 18, Cambridge University Press 1996

Mason, Ian L., ed., *Evolution of Domesticated Animals*, Longman 1984

Mason, Laura, 'Lard', in Davidson, *Companion*, pp.443–4

—, with Catherine Brown, *Traditional Foods of Britain: an Inventory*, Prospect Books 1999

Mitchell, B., and F.C. Robinson, *A Guide to Old English*, 5th ed. Blackwell 1992

Monk, M.A., 'Post-Roman Drying Kilns and the Problem of Function: a Preliminary Statement', in Donnchadh Ó Corráin, ed., *Irish Antiquity: Essays and Studies presented to Professor M.J. Kelly*, Tower Books 1991, pp.216–30

—, 'The Plant Economy and Agriculture of the Anglo-Saxons in Southern Britain, with particular reference to the "Mart" Settlements at Southampton and Winchester', unpublished dissertation, University of Southampton 1977

Morgan, Joan, and Alison Richards, *The Book of Apples*, Ebury Press in association with the Brogdale Horticultural Trust 1993

Morris, Carole A., *Craft, Industry and Everyday Life: Wood and Woodworking in Anglo-Scandinavian and Medieval York*, Archaeology of York 17/13, Council for British Archaeology 2000

Murphy, Peter, *Buttermarket, Ipswich, Suffolk (1AS 3104): (2) Carbonised Loaves*, Ancient Monuments Laboratory Report no. 75/90, English Heritage 1990

Napier, Arthur S., 'Altenglische Miscellen', *Archiv* 84, 1890, pp.322–7

—, *Wulfstan*, Sammlung englischer Denkmäler 4, Berlin 1883

Ohnuki-Tierney, Emiko, *Rice as Self: Japanese Identities Through Time*, Princeton University Press 1993

Paston-Williams, Sara, *The Art of Dining: a History of Cooking and Eating*, National Trust 1993

Payne, Sebastian, 'Animal Husbandry' in Lapidge *et al.*, *Encyclopaedia*, pp.38–9.

Pettit, Edward, ed. and trans., *Anglo-Saxon Remedies, Charms and Prayers from British Library MS Harley 585: the Lacnunga*, Edwin Mellen 2001

Pheifer, J. D., *Old English Glosses in the Épinal–Erfurt Glossary*, Clarendon Press 1974

Plummer, Charles, ed., *Venerabilis Bedae opera historica*, Oxford 1896

Rackham, Oliver, *The History of the Countryside*, Weidenfeld and Nicolson 1995

Renfrew, Jane M., *Palaeoethnobotany: the Prehistoric Food Plants of the Near East and Europe*, Methuen 1973

Reynolds, Peter, *Iron-Age Farm*, British Museum 1979

Riggs, T.J., 'Carrot' in Smartt and Simmonds, *Evolution of Crop Plants*, pp.447–80

—, 'Umbelliferous Minor Crops', in Smartt and Simmonds, *Evolution of Crop Plants*, pp.481–5

Roberts, Charlotte A., 'Malnutrition', in Lapidge *et al.*, *Encyclopaedia*, pp.299–300

Ryder, M.L., *Sheep and Man*, Duckworth 1983

Salisbury, C.R., 'Primitive British Fishweirs', in G.L. Good, R.H. Jones and M.W. Ponsford, eds, *Waterfront Archaeology*, London 1991

Sawyer, P.H., *Anglo-Saxon Charters: an Annotated List and Bibliography*, revised edition by S.E. Kelly, Cambridge 1994 (also available on the internet at www.trin.cam.ac.uk/chartwww)

Seymour, John and Sally, *Self-Sufficiency: the Science and Art of Producing and Preserving your own Food*, Faber 1973

Smartt, J., and N.W. Simmonds, eds, *Evolution of Crop Plants*, 2nd ed. Longman 1995

Stafford, Pauline, 'The Farm of One Night and the Organisation of King Edward's Estates in Domesday Book', *English Historical Review* 33, 1980, pp.491–522

Symons, Thomas, *The Monastic Agreement of the Monks and Nuns of the English Nation*, Nelson 1953

Tangl, Michael, ed., *Die Briefen des heiligen Bonifatius und Lullus*, Monumenta Germaniae Historica, Epistolae Selectae I, Berlin 1916.

Thomas, Hugh, 'Oats', in Smartt and Simmonds, *Evolution of Crop Plants*, pp.132–7

Tomlinson, Philippa, and Allan Hall, *The Archaeobotanical Computer Database (ABCD): a Guide for Users*, Environmental Archaeology Unit, York, revised ed. 1995

Vaughan, J.G., and C.A. Geissler, *The New Oxford Book of Food Plants*, Oxford University Press 1997

Wade-Martins, Peter, *et al.*, *Excavations in North Elmham Park 1967–1972*, 2 vols, East Anglian Archaeology 9, 1980

Wallis, Faith, trans., *Bede: The Reckoning of Time*, Translated Texts for Historians 29, Liverpool University Press 1999

Watkins, Ray, 'Apple and Pear', in Smartt and Simmonds, *Evolution of Crop Plants*, pp.418–22

—, 'Cherry, Plum, Peach, Apricot and Almond', in Smartt and Simmonds, *Evolution of Crop Plants*, pp.423–9

Wellcome MS 46 is edited by Napier, 'Altenglische Miscellen'

Wilson, C. Anne, *Food and Drink in Britain*, Constable 1973

Wilson, D. Gay, 'Plant Remains from the Graveney Boat and the Early History of *Humulus lupulus* L. in Western Europe', *New Phytologist* 75, 1975, pp.133–50

Wilson, David, *Anglo-Saxon Art from the Seventh Century to the Norman Conquest*, Thames and Hudson 1984

Wren, R.C., revised by Elizabeth M. Wilson and Fred J. Evans, *Potter's New Cyclopaedia of Botanical Drugs and Preparations*, C.W. Daniel 1988

Zupitza, Julius, ed., *Ælfrics Grammatik und Glossar*, Berlin 1880

INDEX

Notes: a **bold** page number indicates an illustration.
Plants and animals are listed under their common names.

If you are interested in purchasing other books published by Tempus,
or in case you have difficulty finding any Tempus books in your local bookshop,
you can also place orders directly through our website

www.tempus-publishing.com

or from

BOOKPOST, Freepost, PO Box 29, Douglas, Isle of Man IM99 1BQ
Tel 01624 836000   email bookshop@enterprise.net

South East Essex College
of Arts and Technology, Southend